INSIDE
THE CHEATER'S
MIND

Why He Cheats & Why She Cheats

DR. DENISE
WOOD
&
COLLEEN
HITCHCOCK

LEOPARD SPOT
PRESS

Additional copies of this book are available from the publisher:

©2010 Leopard Spot Press
7117 Cornelia Drive
Edina, MN 55435
www.leopardspot.com

The information in this volume is not intended as a substitute for consultation with healthcare professionals. A qualified professional should evaluate each individual's health concerns.

Printed in the United States of America
First printing: 2010
14 13 12 11 10   5 4 3 2 1

This book is printed on acid-free paper.

Library of Congress Cataloging-in-Publication Data
Wood, Denise, Dr.
Inside the cheater's mind : why he cheats & why she cheats / by Denise Wood & Colleen Hitchcock.
   p. cm.
Includes bibliographical references and index.
ISBN-13: 978-0-9723441-6-6 (trade pbk. : alk. paper)
ISBN-10: 0-9723441-6-0 (trade pbk. : alk. paper)
1. Adultery—United States—Psychological aspects. 2. Adultery—United States—Case studies. 3. Communication in marriage—United States. I. Hitchcock, Colleen. II. Title.
HQ806.W66 2010
306.73'6—dc22
                    2010043178

The case illustrations in this book are based on the author's research and clinical practice. In all instances, names, portions of the story, and identifying information have been changed and/or artistic license used to respect individual privacy.

For more information about the authors or to join their newsletters, visit their websites at: www.drdenisewood.com and www.colleenhitchcock.com.

UPC Bar Code: 0 95333 10001 5

Book cover design by Michael Schwengel
Edited by Renni Browne & Shannon Roberts
Proof-editing by Rich Maguson

*Dedicated to Jim,
Nick & Page, you are
my heart, my love,
my fun.*

*With Love,
Denise*

*For Craig,
my brother,
& my best friend.*

*With love,
Colleen*

CONTENTS

ACKNOWLEDGMENTS

With gratitude to my loving husband, Jim of 13 years and appreciation to my children, Nick, and Page, for letting mommy spend hours on the computer when they wanted to spend family time with me.

I thank my father, Dennis, who taught me to love books and believe in myself. May you rest in peace, daddy; and to my mother, Connie who is my biggest fan. Thank you for telling me I could achieve anything, you always let me follow my dreams.

A loving remembrance for my brother, Scott, who left his life too early. Scott, you are an angel—but always were, even when you were here on Earth.

Bless my sister, Mandee, for her kind heart and inspiring words.

My friends were so helpful and patient with me through out the writing of this book. Thank you—you know who you are.

I thank my co-author, Colleen. I could not have done the book without her; she is truly an inspiration in every sense of the word.

I give great gratitude to God for entering every counseling session with me. We have saved a lot of marriages and relationships together and I depend upon the presence.

With Love,

Denise

With deepest gratitude to Denise, who is a brilliant counselor, great friend, and a super fun co-author. Special thanks to Renni, Shannon, & The Editorial Department for their insightful editing of our book—and Sir Rich of Sir Editor for his proofing.

To my graphics professionals, Mike and Josh; and Sierrah who helps me hold it together at home, you are all gifted geniuses—and are the great kids that I forgot to have. And new friend, Ryan, my book design titan.

And a special astral thanks to the beautiful spirit of my Mom, Eve, who gave us a sign in the writing of this book. I'm proud to be your daughter. And for my Dad, for his loving guidance and who sat me down at 17—and told me I should never break a heart.

You are all beloved,

Colleen

AUTHOR'S PREFACE

"Every time he does this to me, I fall apart," the young mother of two said to me.

Ashley Kelly is an attractive woman with a trim figure and a gorgeous face. But as she sits in my office, her face is pained, her eyes red and swollen with tears. "What did I do wrong? Doesn't he love me? Don't the kids and I make him happy?" She grabbed a wad of Kleenex from the tissue box on the end table.

"This isn't about anything you did wrong, Ashley," I said.

"Damn you, Rick! What is it? What is it? Aren't I good enough in bed?"

Rick, Ashley's husband of six years, stood by the window overlooking the parking lot. He didn't react to his wife. He looked as if he was doing some painful soul-searching, but I could see he was really watching a hot blonde from our building walk to her sports car.

"It's not you, Ashley," I said. "A marriage is a system. When there is cheating, it is usually the breakdown of several issues in the marriage, and it means that both partners need to work hard to save the marriage."

Over the course of my therapy sessions I've noticed repetitive core issues for partners who cheat, issues that seem to be based on their personality traits. Counseling and therapy uncovers issues that drive our dysfunctional behaviors, but no single answer fits all patients. I've discovered each personality cheats for different reasons. This book sheds light on the personality traits and situational reasons behind infidelity issues.

Inside the Cheater's Mind will discuss specific personalities and the motivations they create for cheating. Once the reasons are illuminated, they become an important factor in awakening cheaters to their own motivations. Once the motive is identified, a therapist can create a plan to address the issues, offer the couple solutions for their problems, or simply help the couple discover that the relationship will not work.

I'll be sharing the stories of a number of cheaters I've met through my private practice and my part-time work in prisons. Each story addresses the cheater's personality traits, my assessment based on our sessions, and aspects of the cheater's background to help diagnose the underlying causes of the cheater's infidelity.

Each section has questionnaires and recommendations to help cheaters and their partners deal with infidelity issues. If you're ending your relationship, this book can help you understand what went wrong so you don't draw in the same personality types again and again.

The termination of a relationship with history, love, children, and family is not something I take lightly. I'm married and know first-hand there are good days and bad days in any long-term relationship. I've assisted many couples trying to figure out if they can heal their infidelity issues and go the distance together, or if they must abandon the relationship for their own peace of mind.

I hope this book helps those who have a cheating partner or who may be cheating in their relationship. My wish is that in seeing another's story, you may gain insight into yourself or someone you love.

All these stories were told to me in professional confidence and have been revised so that real people can't be identified. At times my co-author or I have used artistic license to make the scenes come alive for the reader.

I hope this book is of help to you as you decide upon your path.

With love,

Dr. Denise Wood

FROM THE DESK OF DR. DENISE WOOD

It was about ten below zero on a cold Minnesota day, but things were hot in my office. This was a first session with Jason and Raven, a young couple who came to me for marriage counseling. Jason stormed back and forth in my office, red-faced and getting madder by the minute.

"She fucked my best friend, Dr. Wood. It's hopeless—we'll never get over this!" He sat down and shook his head. "This is worse than a death. How does any man get over this?"

I looked over to see Raven squirm in her chair.

"She lied to me, right to my face," Jason said. "I'll never be the same. My marriage will never be the same!"

Raven sat looking at my carpet, expressionless. Jason's contemptuous look was lost on her.

"What were you two thinking? You're just a fucking slut to me. I can't even bear to look at you. You'll shatter our family and lose me over this, so I hope he was worth it, you bitch!"

"Jason, my office is a safe place for both of you and I will not tolerate you verbally abusing your wife no matter how angry you are. The same ground rules will apply to Raven. Is this understood?" Jason reluctantly nodded his head yes.

"All my life I worked my ass off for you and the kids, and this is what I get?" he asked. "Steve is hotter? I don't make enough money? What is it, Raven?"

Raven kept looking down. She had yet to say a word.

"You know what, Raven? I can't stand to be in the same room with you." Jason grabbed his coat and started to leave my office.

"Jason, Raven and you have had a loving relationship in the past, let's stay in therapy to save your marriage," I said. The couple had come this far together and I didn't want to give up this easy.

Jason froze in place and glared at Raven.

"Take a seat, Jason. and let's make sure this never happens again," I said.

He slowly took a seat away from Raven then turned back to me and said, "I'm listening."

Raven finally spoke. "How do I make it better?"

ONCE A CHEATER,
ALWAYS A CHEATER?

Most people know that cheating will hurt their partner and jeopardize their relationship. Yet 74% of men and 68% of women say they would cheat if they knew they'd never be caught.[1]

Infidelity isn't new. Adam may not have cheated on Eve, but history is full of cheating kings from King David to King Henry VIII, cheating politicians, actors and sports figures, celebrities major and minor. Infidelity in some other countries like France and Italy is more accepted—at least, an affair is less likely to break up a marriage.

In the United States the average length of an affair is two years. 53% of marriages end in divorce and 41% admit to either physical or emotional infidelity at some time in their marriage. 57% of men and 54% of women admit to infidelity within relationships. Only 31%, fewer than 1 in 3 marriages, will last after an affair is discovered or admitted. My experience with couples tells me

---

1   http://www.infidelityfacts.com This site contains facts and information on infidelity. The infidelity related information contained on this site has been compiled from numerous sources, such as; university research, psychological surveys, mass public polls, and the recordings of marriage and family counselors.

that this percentage can be increased with therapy and a greater understanding of the root causes of cheating.

In the United States we tend to demonize cheaters, seeing their behavior as a reflection on their moral character. As a doctor of clinical psychology, I believe cheating should be looked at no differently than any other mental health issue. Cheating flags the marriage that it is a broken system, rather than writing it off as a character flaw that can never be fixed and maintained.

No matter how much Americans cheat, monogamy is the societal sexual norm in the United States. Look how angry Americans get at public figures that cheat, from Governor Sanford to Tiger Woods to whoever this week's cheating celebrity may be. For quite a while Bill Clinton was more infamous as a cheater than he was famous as a president.

Why is American society so stuck on monogamy? Most European countries aren't. Why is this? Why is the average American closed to open relationships? We all grow at different rates and evolve into different individuals as we grow. Is the person you made a commitment to ten years ago the same person today? I would think not, nevertheless, most Americans think that life long monogamy makes perfect sense.

Americans are obsessed with famous cheaters. Could it be that something is lacking in our own relationships, so when someone more prestigious falls from grace, we take a certain pride in the fact that our own relationship difficulties aren't yet public knowledge? Should the different phases in life bring about a need for a different mate? We often move on from friends we've outgrown;

yet we're expected to stay true to our mate year after year?

As a Doctor of clinical psychology for a number of years, I've worked with over 350 couples that have suffered infidelity issues. Although my clients are all unique individuals and partnerships, they span a wide variety of issues including gay, straight, bisexual, trans-gender, married, dating, divorcéd, single-but-wants-to-be-married, and married-but-wants-to-be-single. This book is the result of the main conclusions that transpired after the therapy sessions.

Most couples that come to me with infidelity issues tell me they "want to make their relationship work again." Next they tell me their sex life was nonexistent or unsatisfactory prior to the infidelity. Which is interesting, because they both knew there was something missing from their relationship yet chose not to go to a therapist for help. They often tell me they used to have rock-star sex when they first met. What are the reasons why and how the great sex ended?

Other reasons for infidelity are: "We got too comfortable with one another." "It didn't seem worth the effort." "We were too tired." "We were too busy." "We had kids." "She cheated on me five years ago and I swore I'd never have sex with her again." "The dog sleeps in our bed, and so does the cat sometimes." "Our kids still sleep in the bed." I work too hard." "He's always gone on business trips." "I'm too tired." "I was in a car crash three years ago and have incredible back pain." "I have no sexual desire any more." "We love each other, sex is just boring." "We feel almost too close, like I'm having sex with my brother or my sister." "We just stay together because of the house, money, and the kids." Etc.

Most of these couples admitted they loved or at least valued the stability of their marriage, the warmth, the connection, the memories, but they miss the thrill of a new relationship. They liked the familiarity of their partnership but wanted the excitement of the unknown.

Do you have to go outside the marriage for great sex? Could it be that you want what you already have but don't know how to achieve the balance of a good relationship with a good mate and sexual partner in the real world? Infidelity occurs in a fantasy world where deceit and white lies become your best friend and guilt accompanies you every step of the way.

Monogamy is the reality where two people learn about commitment and real love, and your best friend accompanies you every step of the way. This book can help you become the couple you have always wanted to be if that's in the cards for you. Not the couple that pretends to be happy but a couple that's truly happy. If this isn't in the cards for you, this book can help you recognize that reality and get out.

Is there help for the people who cheat? Absolutely.

I do believe that cheaters are responsible for their own actions, but we need to look at people who cheat as needing help. Often cheating is accompanied by deeper issues and the cheater has other emotional baggage from the past that impacts their present relationships.

Cheaters must be assessed as individuals with their own set of issues that do not involve just cheating. A serial cheater may love their significant other very much, however they may have other deep-seated issues that prevents them from a monogamous relationship.

Some cheating is not physical, but strictly emotional. In fact emotional cheating may even be harder to repair in a relationship than the physical act of cheating. Keep in mind that no individual goes through life unscathed. If you are cheating, or keep choosing partners who are always cheating on you, and desire to be in a monogamous relationship, this book is for you.

If a person you know had schizophrenia, depression, bipolar disorder, anxiety, or other mental health issues; would you strike out with anger or try to get them some help? Some reasons for cheating may be just that deep. So go inside the cheater's mind with me to understand the numerous personality cheaters and situational cheaters.

REASONS SOME INDIVIDUALS MAY CHEAT

So why do cheaters do it? If infidelity has just happened in your relationship, try to step back from your friction and look at other relationships to help you to understand it more objectively. Let's look at a few of the many cheating scenarios possible:

1. The cheater may have a frontal lobe head injury or Adult Attention Deficit Hyperactivity Disorder, both of which tend to make people more impulsive.
2. The cheater may be addicted to sex—sexual addiction is a real disorder.
3. The cheater may have a personality disorder that leads to the behavior.
4. The cheater may feel alone and isolated when with their partner.
5. The cheater who's watching porn alone, visiting strip clubs, or using prostitutes may not feel this is cheating.
6. The cheater may be crying out for help.
7. The cheater may want to get caught.

8. The cheater may have low self-esteem and be trying to overcompensate with multiple sexual partners.

9. The cheater may be unhappy with some important aspect of the relationship and unable to communicate about it. Or communication was tried and ignored.

10. The cheater may be an emotional cheater and think you won't be affected by a non-sexual relationship with another.

11. The cheater may be addicted to drugs or alcohol, which impaired judgment when the cheating began and is now compounding the problem.

12. The cheater may have fallen in love with the other man or woman and eventually crossed the line.

13. The cheater may actually need therapy for core issues and be looking to another for help and/or happiness.

14. The cheater may be an obsessive thrill-seeker and enjoy the adrenaline rush from undercover romance.

15. The cheater may have experienced the loss of a loved one, gone through a traumatic event or life change, and turn to someone outside the marriage for comfort if the partner doesn't seem supportive.

16. The cheater may be trying to even the score if the partner has cheated.

17. The cheater may be attracted to someone who unlike the partner shares his or her sexual orientation.
18. The cheater may have certain sexual fetishes or preferences he or she doesn't think the partner will understand.
19. The cheater may no longer be sexually attracted to the partner.
20. The cheater—especially a male cheater— may feel that his behavior is normal, an idea that may be reinforced by other men.
21. The cheater may be trying to fill a narcissistic void by cheating.
22. The cheater may be tired of fighting with the partner and turn elsewhere for a harmonious relationship.
23. The cheater may feel as if he/she no longer has anything in common with the partner.
24. The cheater may have a much higher sex drive than the partner.

PERSONALITY

CHEATERS

TYPES OF CHEATERS

People often believe they can lump all cheaters into one big he's-a-dirt bag/she's-a-slut category. I trust *Inside the Cheater's Mind* will dispel this myth. I don't condone cheating because I've seen far too many people deeply hurt by this type of betrayal, but understanding rather than condemnation is more likely to save the relationship.

As I observed so many cheating relationships over the years, I began to see situational patterns and recurring personality issues. I found common threads in numerous relationships and concluded that different people cheat for different reasons.

When I discovered core issues, I was able to place cheaters in different categories and plan a treatment program to address their specific issues. If you've cheated on your partner, or your partner has cheated on you, understanding the kind of cheater your partner may be can be a valuable first step. Although some personality issues may overlap at times, knowing what qualities a client displays has helped tremendously with the treatment and healing process. It also helps the cheater's partner gain insight into his or her behavior.

My premise is that cheaters fall into two categories:

1. Personality Cheaters—These people often have a difficult time in therapy, and their cheating is more ingrained. Usually they have to undergo a more intense treatment program to deal with their personality issues as well as the infidelity these issues encourage.
2. Situational Cheaters—These cheaters are typically easier to work with because if it weren't for certain circumstances, they might not have cheated.

Personality Cheaters

The Impulsive Cheater

Our first Personality Cheater is the Impulsive Cheater. These men or women tend to get bored easily, may lack attention to detail or have trouble completing a task. Often they appear to have difficulty listening or pay-ing attention to others. They may do poorly in school or structured work atmospheres. They also may have a difficult time dealing with rigid or structured home environments.

These cheaters may rebel against routine. They may be prone to drug or alcohol addiction. They may have no intention of cheating, but when temptation arises, their lack of impulse control leads them to infidelity.

Narcissistic Cheater

The second Personality Cheater is the Narcissistic Cheater. This cheater is highly self-focused, in serious need of admiration, and becomes uncomfortable when not the center of attention. Narcissistic cheaters often exaggerate the expression of emotion and may consistently present themselves with an air of grandiosity.

Narcissistic cheaters don't often end up in therapy—it's everybody else who's out of whack, not them—but if they do, they'll want the *best* doctor of psychology they can find. Narcissistic cheaters have a strong sense of entitlement and are often preoccupied with ideas of unlimited success, power, brilliance, or beauty. They themselves are often attractive, charming, and successful.

Although these cheaters seem confident, their self-esteem is actually very fragile. They may discuss their own issues or concerns in great detail but lack sensitivity to the needs of others. For instance, their perceived needs are more important than whatever pain they may cause through their infidelity.

Since narcissists are unlikely to seek therapy, the prospects are dim for a successful monogamous relationship with this type of cheater. Should they actually agree to seek therapy they'll have to spend a lot of time learning what their partners need if a monogamous relationship is to have any chance of succeeding.

Pathological Cheater

The Pathological Cheater lacks remorse and has little respect for others. These cheaters often lie to their partners and may seem to enjoy the con. They often lack forethought and apparently feel entitled to do whatever they want, regardless of how their actions are perceived by society. Although they often seem overly opinionated, self-assured, or cocky, the pathological cheater may exude a superficial charm.

Not surprisingly, they tend to be irresponsible or exploitative in sexual relationships and may never have sustained a monogamous relationship. Substance abuse and impulse control disorders are common among pathological cheaters, who often see themselves as free spirits. This type of cheater may need a number of therapy sessions with their partner before they can even grasp the implications of their actions.

Charismatic Cheater

The most striking characteristic of the Charismatic Cheater is pervasive attention-seeking behavior. In fact, these cheaters are downright uncomfortable when they're not the center of attention. They may behave in a provocative or seductive manner and tend to charm new acquaintances with their enthusiasm and flirtatiousness. (The charismatic cheater may be hard to tell from a narcissistic cheater.) But this provocative behavior is not just directed toward a single potential sexual partner. Charismatic cheaters often share their sexual energy and time with a number of people. There's a strong element of compulsion to their cheating.

Their emotions shift rapidly depending on the time and place. A long-term relationship may be neglected in order to make room for a number of potential new romantic encounters. Charismatic cheaters usually need sex rehabilitation therapy for a number of months before they can entertain any hope for a stable monogamous relationship.

Escapist Cheater

The Escapist Cheater is often preoccupied with perfection at others' expense. These cheaters typically try to maintain control over their partner and may search for someone they *can* control if their partners aren't acquiescent enough to suit them. They're prone to attention to detail and may endlessly nag a partner over a perceived weakness in his or her ability to care for the cheater, for themselves, or for family members.

Escapist cheaters may claim to be rigid about morality and ethics, cheat, and deal with guilt later. They tend to be critical about their own mistakes as well as the mistakes of others. They may show emotion in a highly controlled manner but tend to be preoccupied with their partner's imperfections. Escapist cheaters often have affairs with people who are similar to them in nature and tend to seek comfort in someone they perceive as perfect. Thus they may obsess about a prospect, since they're forever on the lookout for the perfect person to take the stress out of their imperfect (or chaotic) life or their imperfect partnership.

Down-low Cheater

The Down-low Cheater is either gay or bisexual but hides this sexual preference even from his partner.

Whatever the Down-low cheater decides to do—stay in the marriage or partnership, leave to live alone, leave to be with a lover of the same sex—the couple will benefit from therapy, as there are likely to be feelings of hurt and rejection on both sides.

If you're with a down-low cheater and your condition of satisfaction in the partnership is monogamy, accept the reality of your partner's sexual preference and get out or stay in knowing that you may have to share your partner with members of the opposite sex.

Puppeteer Cheater

The Puppeteer Cheater wants to establish control in his/her relationships, so it's not surprising that these people tend to cheat with a sexual partner who is younger, vulnerable, or naive. They may hold a position of respect such as counselor or religious leader, which they abuse in order to prey on those in their care. There is often a big power differential between puppeteer cheaters and their sexual partners, and this personality type may seek other sexual relationships if the object of their affection acts out or defies them.

Puppeteer cheaters may seem charming and go to extensive lengths to nurture and support the object of their affection. Once they obtain their object of affection they can be verbally, physically, or sexually abusive and may use this behavior as a means of control.

The puppeteer often seeks sexual partners who lack self-esteem or are otherwise down and out—a bereavement group, for example, might be a hunting ground. Puppeteer cheaters frequently have multiple "relationships," all of which are as superficial as the puppeteer's charm and caring.

Addictive Cheater

The Addictive Cheater is addicted to cheating—among other things. These cheaters tend to gamble, shop, or have other hobbies on which they spend an unhealthy amount of time. They often have issues with drug and alcohol abuse.

Many of these cheaters, especially men, are addicted to strip clubs and/or pornography and will seek out like-minded guys to cheat with them. Addictive cheaters will almost certainly cheat again, even if caught, unless they seek help for their addiction as well as their addictive sexual behavior.

Monogamy for this type of cheater is a long shot, but with hard work and a desire to change, it's possible.

Dependent Cheater

The Dependent Cheater lacks self-esteem and often goes to extensive lengths to obtain nurturance and support from others. The need to maintain a relationship will often end in an unhealthy power differential.

When dependent cheaters feel their relationship may end or their partner is ignoring them, they become desperate to find another relationship to fill a possible void. They may go from one cheating relationship to another just to avoid being alone.

Because they so often have very low self-esteem, dependent cheaters typically don't trust their own judgment. They often submit to their lover's needs even if they tend to be unreasonable. They often end up in affairs for fear of saying no, as their self-esteem can't handle rejection after the fact.

1

IMPULSIVE CHEATER
FEMALE

Tanya

Tanya Whitehall dropped off the kids for the night with Dorothy, her mother.

"Tanya, be sweet to Sean—he's a great catch," her mom said. "Don't miss the boat like I did. It would be good for Dominic to have a real father figure."

"He sees his father."

"Sure, on his birthday? You know you can't count on Jerrol to come through. He's not an active dad—you see him when you see him."

"So what? They see one of the baby daddies around."

"Tanya, you've got three kids from three daddies, you don't need to collect the daddies. Be done with the no-goods that come in and out of your life. Find a good man like Sean and create a nice family life for yourself."

"Okay, I will, I will."

"I know that tone, Tanya, you aren't taking me seriously. Sean works for IBM, he's a good-looking church-going guy, drug-free, smart, and he even has money to take you to Europe. I didn't raise you to be no dumb girl. Get smart here."

"I'm not a dumb girl, Mama."

"Really? You got one in prison, another's a little crook, and a third one's a two-timer. You find yourself a good family man and settle down."

"Okay, okay, I got it, Mama. Sean's is taking me somewhere nice tonight. How do I look?"

"Real pretty, honey. You always look pretty."

"Thanks, Mama." She hugged her mother tight. "And thanks for keeping the kids all night. Now he's here, I better go."

She ran out to Sean's car, a blue Lexus. He went around to the passenger side and opened her door. At a high-priced restaurant known for its great steaks and seafood Tanya ordered the lobster dinner and Sean didn't flinch. After their wine was poured, he reached over and took her hand.

"I'm a dreamer, Tanya. I wondered if you would dream with me."

"I can do that." Tanya smiled big.

"You know I just bought a house last month, haven't shown it to you because I had some remodeling done. I'm having the hardwood floors redone and finishing off a fifth bedroom."

"Five bedrooms? It must be big."

"Thirty-five hundred square feet in Highlands," he said.

"Do you know I've dreamed of living in Highlands?"

"It's great, but it would be better with you and your

kids there." He was looking at her so intently she wasn't surprised when he said, "Tanya, I have an important question for you."

"Yes?" She leaned forward in her seat.

"If you were in love, would you say goodbye to the other men you've had in your life and be true to just one man—like me, for instance?"

Tanya looked at his face, so earnest, so full of love for her.

"I know I would. If it was a man like you, Sean."

"Then I have an even more important question for you."

This was it! Sean stood up and went around to her side and got down on one knee. He reached in his pocket and pulled out a ring box.

"Tanya, I love you. I want to love you forever and love and take care of your children, too. I'll be there for them—and for you—every day. I want to be the man you can all count on. Tanya, will you marry me?"

He said it with so much love that Tanya felt her eyes filling up. She looked at the huge bling in the open box. Such a beautiful diamond—it had to be two carats.

"Oh Sean, I love you too. Yes! Yes, I'll marry you," And he slid the ring on her finger. When they kissed, the whole restaurant applauded.

After dinner Tanya invited Sean back to her small Section 8 apartment and made love to him a couple of times. He fell asleep until 3:00 am. When he woke up he heard a mouse scurry across the floor and decided he'd stay the rest of the night in his own bed at the new house. He couldn't wait to spend nights there with Tanya.

He kissed her goodnight. She woke up and held onto him.

"Sean, I will never, ever take your ring off. I promise."

Sean drove home from Tanya's a happy man. He had a fiancée, an instant family, a promotion at IBM with a hefty salary increase, and a beautiful clean new house.

At 4:00 am Tanya's phone rang.

"Baby? I need you," Jerrol said. "I just got out."

"Too late for a booty call, Jerrol, go to bed." In fifteen minutes he knocked on her door. She looked out the peephole.

"Go away, I'm sleeping," she said.

"I got to tell you something. It's about Spanky."

Spanky was one of Tanya's best friends. She took off her engagement ring and hid it in her drawer. Jerrol had taken some of her jewelry before, and besides, she didn't want him asking questions. She opened the door.

"What about Spanky?"

"Spanky got arrested."

"For what?"

"Dope."

"Is someone going to bail him out?"

"His mom will borrow off somebody." Jerrol stepped inside and started to take off his shirt.

"You aren't staying here, get out," she said.

He grabbed her and held her tight. "I missed you, Tanya."

"We're done, Jerrol."

"You'll never be done with me—the sex is too good, baby. We're like salt and pepper, we just go together."

He kissed her like he missed her, and she let him. Before she knew it they were in bed together.

He was even stronger than she remembered—or maybe after Sean's smaller, wiry frame Jerrol's body was just that much more noticeable. She loved his masculine scent, and when she held on to him she felt like she was with a wild stallion. Jerrol rode her against the wall, on the dresser, on the bed—so many positions her head was spinning. She loved it. The sex was primitive, exhausting, and God, how she loved it.

That morning, coming back from the bathroom, she watched his nude body move across the room. He had the body of an athlete and she appreciated watching him move.

"Oh, how did I miss this?" he said.

"Miss what?"

"This nice Rolex here." He slid it on to see how it looked on him. "This puppy looks real. Is this for me?"

"No, give it to me," she said. He just kept admiring the watch.

She heard her front door open with a key. Sean appeared at the bedroom door.

"I forgot my watch—"

"Sorry, man." Jerrol walked over to Sean and took the watch off slow.

"Damn, Tanya, am I second shift?" Sean looked like he'd been kicked in the stomach. "Where's the ring?"

"Sean, I was trying to protect it," she said.

"I see that. Where is it?"

She went to the dresser and pulled out the ring.

"Oh, man, you thought you were going to marry Tanya?" Jerrol laughed. "She ain't a keeper. You just come around sometimes, that's all."

Sean took the ring. "I made a mistake."

"I'm sorry, Sean."

"I believed you when you said you could settle down."

"I could. I really—"

"No, you can't. Not even for a few hours, you can't."

Sean never called Tanya again. He met someone at church and was married a year later.

Tanya had a fourth child from a man she knew for only a week. He disappeared before she even learned she was pregnant. After that baby arrived, there were no more marriage offers for Tanya.

Tanya's Meeting:

Tanya sauntered into my office. Very attractive and young—twenty-five, I was to learn.

"Hi, just so you know, I don't want to be here, but my mom made me come. She thinks I need help. Mom's husband said he would pay for the sessions, what a sucker."

"Please have a seat," I said.

"Okay." She plopped down on my couch with her arms folded. "So what do we do now?"

"Why does your mother want you to see a therapist?"

"She says I pick the wrong men."

"Do you?"

Tanya looked at me and shrugged.

"I have AIDS," she said.

"Are you frightened?" I asked.

"I know lots of people with AIDS and they're fine. The doc said it's in remission right now. Mom can always take the kids if I croak." I saw her look down at her phone.

"Hey, sorry to cut the session short, but I've got to run. Jerrol just got out of prison and that slacker Spanky forgot to pick him up. See you next week, same time, okay?" And she ran out the door.

Tanya's Background:

Tanya's father went to prison when she was five years old. She remembered visiting him there twice.

She said that one time the guards wouldn't let them in to visit her father because they said her mother's outfit was too revealing. Tanya didn't know what that meant at the time, but her mother was wearing a mini-skirt with a tank top. She said her mom cried and cried because it took three hours to drive to the prison. She and her brother just fell asleep in the back seat of the car listening to her mom's sobbing.

According to Tanya, she never really knew her father because he was always doing some business deals. She said she always had a lot of "uncles" around the house. She and her brother would try to listen to her father and uncles when they were talking, but if they were caught they'd get a whipping.

The second time they went to visit her father in prison; a woman was leaving just as they walked in.

According to Tanya, her mother stormed over to her father, said something about divorce papers, and stormed out. Tanya looked back and saw her father and the other prisoners laughing at her mother.

Tanya said she stayed awake this time and her mother cried all the way home. After that her mother married a car mechanic, who Tanya said was always boring but always home, and nice to her and her brother. Her mother made her promise she would marry a nice man with a decent job. "I've never been interested in nice men," Tanya told me. "Boring and too easy to play."

Tanya's Assessment:

Tanya has a self-defeating attitude in which she manifests herself as a self-destructive adolescent. When life doesn't transpire the way she wants, she tends to act out even more. Although she understands that certain men aren't good for her, she continues to hang out with them, have unprotected sex with them, and have children with them. Tanya derives such self-worth as she has and such meaning as she can put together from her superficial sexual encounters.

She continues to have unprotected sex into her twenties, unworried about any consequences of her promiscuous affairs. Her affect, quality of speech, and grasp of reality all appear to be questionable. Any number of disorders may be present or develop, individually or simultaneously. Her behavior is certainly aberrant and erratic more often than not.

Tanya's Recommendations:

- Tanya needs therapy to find out what emotional void she's trying to fill with her self-destructive behavior. Therapy can help her address specific self-destructive behaviors, such as why she keeps choosing to be in relationships in which she is demeaned instead of respected.
- Tanya should take a birth control class, as she needs to take responsibility for her actions and start using protective sexual measures.
- She needs special training on having sex while HIV positive, to learn to protect her partners.
- Therapy and counseling can help Tanya find partners who strengthen her ego and address other life problems.
- She needs to become more of a role model for her children.
- She needs to work on her low self-esteem.
- She needs to acknowledge that she has sexual issues that are preventing her from an intimate relationship.
- Family therapy would be beneficial as well, because Tanya's mother appears to be an enabler.
- Tanya needs to find extra-curricular activates that don't revolve around sex.

Tools: Are you an Impulsive Cheater?

1. Do you often find yourself having unprotected or risky sex with a stranger?
2. Do you use sex as a tool to get what you want from certain people?
3. Do you fail to develop sexual relationships appropriate to your chronological age?
4. Do you find yourself with sexual partners who don't respect you?
5. Do you feel emotionally distant from your partner or mate?
6. At times do you feel as if the only reason you want your partner around is for sex?
7. Do you find that you're disrespectful to your lover(s)?
8. Does your attitude toward sex cause significant impairment in your relationships?
9. Do you find that you're unable to sustain a long-lasting, intimate, sexual relationship?

If you answered yes to four or more of the above questions you may be an Impulsive Cheater.

2

IMPULSIVE CHEATER
MALE

Mick

Mick walked into the strip club.

"The usual?" asked the bartender.

"Yeah." Mick threw down a hundred-dollar bill. "Start a tab and send Angela over."

"Sure." The bartender set down a whiskey straight. "I saw your fight at the arena the other night. You kicked ass."

"Thanks," Mick said. He lifted his glass to drink and poured the liquor in crookedly on the right side of his mouth. His lips and the left side of his face were swollen and his eye was puffed out like an orange, the skin split below his brow.

"Doctor told me I better quit fighting or I won't be able to remember my own name. Just a few more knocks on the noggin, he said. What do those quacks know anyway?"

"Looks like your girl's arrived," said the bartender.

Angela sauntered up and started dancing for Mick on the stage.

"No, not here. Let's go in the back room," Mick said. Angela followed him back, and he watched her take off her bra and threw it to the side. Her hard nipples aroused him and he impulsively pushed her down on a couch. Mick began to feel her up.

"You aren't supposed to touch me," Angela said trying to push him off her, but he was stronger and holding her down with all his weight.

"You get more money if you let me," he said throwing bills from his jacket near her.

"Get off her, Mick," the bouncer said pulling the boxer from his struggling prey. "You can't touch the strippers. Get out of here."

"She wanted me," Mick said. "Come on, Frank, she's just a whore. Who cares?"

"I do. If this place closes, I don't have a job. Now get out and stay out."

"Screw that—I don't need this bullshit." Mick grabbed the bartender by the shirt.

"You want to call the cops? Do that and I'll beat the shit out of you, punk. You think I'm scared to go back to the slammer? I run that place."

Mick looked at the bartender and thought he had smirk on his face. He knew he could wipe that look off his face. He felt the bartender's heart pounding. Mick wasn't in the heavyweight division for nothing.

He punched the bartender in the face and walked out the back door. The bouncer came after him. Mick turned around and punched him twice in the face before the bouncer fell to his knees. Then he walked into a nightclub across the street.

A girl wearing a skin-tight dress slithered over.

"I know who you are. You're the boxer guy, I saw you fight the other night. You're really strong." She stumbled back into a chair.

"Oops," she said, giggling. She wasn't his type, but she wore a low cut v-neck that showed off impressive assets.

"You party?" She took some cocaine out of her purse.

"I sure do." Mick grabbed her ass with one hand and slid his other down her dress. "Let's go to my place."

Mick woke up in the middle of the night and looked around his trailer. His head was throbbing. There were empty whiskey bottles and cocaine vials on the table. The last thing he remembered was having sex with the woman from the bar before he fell asleep.

He looked over at her, repulsed by her large frame, sagging face, and straggly brown hair.

"Hey." He shook her. "Get out of here."

The woman looked up at him, startled.

"How am I supposed to get home?"

"I don't give a shit how you get home." Mick picked up her clothes and threw them out the trailer door. "Do I look like a taxi driver?"

He could hear the woman crying outside, so he shut the window. He got back in bed and fell back to sleep.

His girlfriend of four years, Cat, let herself in with her key. It took only a few seconds to see another woman's bra on the kitchen table.

"What the hell is this?" Cat screamed. "I work a double shift at the hospital and you have some slut in the trailer again?"

"I don't know what you're talking about." He sat up.

"This!" Cat held up the bra. "This is our home, Mick. You better explain yourself."

"I gave some dude the keys to the trailer so he could fuck some slut without his wife knowing," Mick said.

"How stupid do you think I am? You really think I'm going to believe that?" She grabbed her suitcase. "This is it—I'm not taking your shit anymore!" She threw an empty whiskey bottle at him.

"Leave the car keys," Mick said as dodged the flying bottle aimed at his face.

"That's it? Four years, and all you say is leave the fucking car keys?"

"Okay, bye, bitch. Leave the car keys." Mick said.

"I can't believe I wasted all this time on a no-good cheating asshole," Cat said under her breath as she stormed outside.

Mick lit a cigarette. Damn. Cat was probably the best woman he'd ever had. He snorted some coke. Cat walked back in to pick up her jewelry box. He watched her bend over the bottom drawer and admired her perfect ass.

He grabbed her and slid his hands down her body.

"Come on, baby, don't do this. I just miss you when you're not around," he said. "Come to bed."

"No way," Cat said. "Not until you explain that bra."

"I told you, Lenny brought some chick in here. Now don't punish me for telling you the truth, and don't get Lenny in trouble with Dora."

"Okay, but I still don't know if I believe you." Cat reluctantly got in bed with Mick.

Mick's Meeting:

"I come home from a double shift and first thing I see is some bra on the table. When I confronted Mick he told me Lenny used our place to have an affair, and I shouldn't tell his wife. The next morning I call Dora and find out Lenny was passed out at their house all night. So Mick lied to me."

Mick is sitting across from me, smiling like some kid with his hand in the cookie jar

"He demands my fidelity, then he fucks around. We're not married, I can leave whenever I want."

"Doc, I don't want that." Mick looked at Cat and smiled. "I like being around her. She's the best girl ever."

"He's trying to charm you," Cat said. "I want to be married to a man I can trust. This session won't do any good, because Mick's a cheater and he'll always be a cheater. Men don't change like that." Cat snapped her fingers in the air.

"There's no chance, Dr. Wood. You can probably do that with some of these suburban husbands, but Mick's got too much tomcat in him. He's always on the prowl. First chance he gets, his pants are around his ankles."

"Mick be straight with me. I have worked in the prison system for years and know when I am being played. From what I have heard from both of you is that you cheat on your girlfriend every chance you get. It sounds as if you are disrespectful and abusive to women. That said I advise that you no longer interact with women until you undergo individual therapy and learn how to treat women in a respectful manner no woman deserves to be denigrated that way," he said.

"What do I have to do, Doc? Are you saying that there is no help for me and I can never be with Cat?"

"This will be a challenge, however you have to work on getting yourself healthy first before you can be in a committed relationship because you're too abusive and disrespectful to your partner. I recommend that the two of you split up for now. When you're ready to have a relationship that is not abusive then you can start dating again."

Mick's Background:

Mick grew up on the streets. He's been in several bar brawls over the years, thanks to the chip he wears on his shoulder. It should also be noted that as a boxer Mick has multiple head injuries that could have caused him to act even more impulsively, particularly if he had frontal lobe damage.

Mick's Assessment:

My assessment of Mick is that he is an impulsive cheater. That is, he literally "takes a female" if he perceives an opportunity. It won't matter if she is saying, 'no' while he makes his advances. There's little regard for boundaries, either those of his partner or of the person with whom he cheats. Once the idea is set in motion, he may take advantage of his object of sexual desire.

In treatment Mick had to work on his understanding

and perceptions about women. The male impulsive cheater feels a strong need to denigrate women, and the cheater doesn't know why. The problem may stem from something experienced in the cheater's childhood or youth, such as watching his father denigrate his mother or other women. The impulsive cheater should seek therapy to find out the initial problem. Specifically identifying the problem will help to determine the solution through therapy.

If you have continuing sexual thoughts about other women/men, tell your therapist, so you can work on the issue and then bring your partner into therapy sessions to work on your relationship. A counselor or therapist can coach couples working on their relationship in ways to deal with potentially inflammatory issues.

Mick's Recommendations:

- Mick needs to be out of his relationship with Cat until he becomes mentally healthy, respectful, and non-abusive in his relationships.
- Mick should be assessed for medication that would help him control his anger and impulsivity.
- He will benefit from individual therapy with a female therapist, since he'll have to learn how to react to females with a certain amount of respect.
- He should be assessed by a neurologist, due to multiple head traumas.

- Group therapy will help him learn how his actions affect others.
- Mick should take an Anger Management course, mandated by the courts if necessary.
- Mick needs to be assessed and treated for illicit drug and alcohol abuse issues.
- Mick should be assessed for adult attention deficit disorder.

Tools: Are you an Impulsive Cheater?

1. Do you find yourself continually distracted by thoughts of sex or sexual activity?
2. Are you unable to concentrate for any length of time without sexual thoughts interfering?
3. Do you experience a flight of sexual thoughts that continue even when you try to put them out of your mind?
4. Have you experienced an increase in goal-directed sexual activity? Do you sometimes find that you'll try anything to get sex?
5. Do you have trouble seeing a member of the opposite sex as anything but a sexual object?
6. Do you have excessive involvement in pleasure-oriented sexual activities, which continues to increase?
7. Have you regularly experienced psychomotor sexual agitation if you don't get the sexual pleasure you desire?
8. Have you lost a job or been in trouble with the law due to sexual activities such as sex

with prostitutes? Have you been held legally accountable for aggressive behavior toward a sexual object, such as having a restraining order issued against you?

9. Do you tend to dismiss or not care about the long-term consequences of a sexual action (such as jail)?

10. Do you sometimes experience a sense of loss of control when seeking sexual activity?

11. Do you display lack of concern for safety when seeking sexual pleasure (for example, not wearing a condom when with prostitutes)?

If you answered yes to five or more of these questions, you may be an impulsive cheater.

3

NARCISSISTIC CHEATER
MALE

Jack

The whole bed was wet and smelled like sex. Jack glanced down the length of Vanessa's body.

God, she was beautiful from any angle.

Vanessa started kissing him. His mind drifted, and he felt himself getting excited again. He looked at his watch.

"Damn," he said, "I'm late."

Vanessa laughed and rolled over, straddling him.

"Isn't three times enough for you?" he asked.

"Not when four is there for the taking."

"I have to go."

"Your loss," she said.

He watched without daring to blink as she glided to the shower.

"Jack, aren't you coming?" She began to soap her body with the shower door open.

In a moment his hands were in her suds. They made love under the warm shower jets, Vanessa holding him tightly and moaning in his ear. Suddenly she turned, giggled, and rubbed her sudsy bottom against him.

He loved to hear her laugh. He loved how she looked when she was wet. He loved the way she smelled, the way her body felt, her free spirit.

Vanessa had a playful fun quality that made him explode with happiness. She was a natural high. Tearing himself away from her was hard.

He stepped out of the shower, and she wiped him off with a plush red towel. Never had such a simple act felt so loving to Jack.

He tried to put his clothes on while she kissed him. She followed him to the door, kissing him over and over again, and he couldn't stop kissing her back no matter how hard he tried. She felt his zipper and winked at him.

Damn! He was hard again. She knew he couldn't get enough of her.

Finally she said," Get out of here," and spanked him on the ass.

Jack bent down for a longer kiss, then stared into her eyes to capture the moment. Finally he ran down her townhouse steps and jumped into his car. He pushed the pedal to the floor, praying for a cop-free drive.

The forty-five minute canyon drive home seemed torturous. Jack didn't want to go back to Megan. Last time he cheated he really hurt her, and he'd sworn on a Bible he'd never do it again. He was so sure he had himself under control this time....

Jack remembered the day Vanessa walked into the office building, the new head of the financial department. She had an MBA from Harvard, and office gossip said her father had gotten her the job because he was well connected and had "old money."

None of that mattered to Jack. She was strikingly beautiful with long well toned legs and expensively streaked blond hair. He wanted her.

Jack's buddy Eddie nudged him while he admired her curves.

"Dude, don't even go there. She's Beverly Hills. You can't afford to look at her. Besides, Megan just about killed herself last time."

"You prick—a guy can dream," Jack said.

Vanessa was a challenge. He was already wondering what she thought of him.

She smiled in his direction once in a while, and every smile made him want more.

She was articulate yet unpretentious. She walked with incredible confidence. Jack's heart raced every time she passed.

She had a French impressionist painting hanging on the wall in her office. He Googled the artist and struck up his first conversation over the art piece.

"I understand this painter is a descendant of an artist who used to paint horses for the King of France," Jack said.

She tilted her head.

"Reminds me of Toulouse Lautrec meets Monet, with more energy and spirit."

"You know, that's really an astute perception," Vanessa said. She talked about meeting the artist when she was in Paris, then said, "I had a really rough week,

Jack. Would you like to grab a quick drink with me?"

"Sure." Jack looked at his watch. Megan was expecting him home in fifteen minutes.

At the corner bar they talked like colleagues, yet their body language was anything but business. Vanessa crossed and uncrossed her legs, which made her skirt slide up. Somehow an extra button opened on her blouse, and Jack was tall enough to see the black silk lace trim on her camisole.

She slid a cocktail straw between her lips.

They touched often. He moved in sync with a hand on her back, around her shoulder, or on her arm as they talked. A few times he moved so that when she turned, her breasts grazed the back of his hand.

"I have an early presentation tomorrow morning, I better go," she said.

"I'll hail you a cab."

Waiting for the cab, Jack leaned over and gave her a kiss. She kissed him back—wow, did she kiss him back.

Vanessa whispered in Jack's ear. "If you can kiss me like that, then I can't wait...."

Jack got in his car and drove home, reliving the kiss, the teasing, and the sexual anticipation he'd felt with Vanessa. Just thinking about her kept him aroused the whole way home—until he pulled up at his driveway.

Megan met him at the door and gave him a huge kiss.

"Sorry I'm late," he said. "What was that for?"

"For being fabulous," she said. "I made your favorite—Porterhouse steak with your red wine."

Not the entrance he expected.

"Do you notice anything different about me?" she asked.

"Your hair is shorter? You bought a new outfit? You worked out today?"

"No, silly." She put her arms around him. "We're pregnant."

Jack paled. Megan took his hand and led him to their bedroom.

"My sister is giving me her baby bed, and Mom's coming the first few weeks after the baby's born," she said. "Jack, isn't it exciting? You're going to be a dad!"

Jack's Meeting:

Megan and Jack came to see me for couple's therapy. When Jack called, he said his partner had issues that were causing problems in their relationship. Megan sat on the couch. Jack strutted around my office, looking at the degrees on my wall.

"So, Jack, what do you hope to get out of therapy?" I asked.

"I want Megan to get better, of course. She's ruining us with this depression bullshit. I can't help it if women go crazy over me—what am I supposed to do, put a bag over my head?"

"Jack, people often bring someone in so I can fix them. But they themselves may also have issues that—"

"Hold on, doc, I just had an epiphany. Maybe we could put a GPS chip in me, so Megan won't have a meltdown every time I leave the house."

Jack's Background:

Jack is a narcissistic cheater who doesn't care about anyone's feelings but his own. When he starts pursuing and eventually beds a new woman any thought of how this will affect Megan or their future relationship goes out the window.

It's not unusual for narcissistic cheaters to become so involved in their own desires that they're oblivious to the needs of others. This cheater's confident, charming facade typically masks a sense of falseness or emptiness caused by a deeply hidden but crippling low self-esteem. They may present a defensive front of self-sufficiency, vanity, and superiority, often displaying a grandiose ego. Jack seems to be in need of constant admiration and displays a strong sense of entitlement.

Jack told me that his mother is an oncologist who graduated from Harvard medical school. Jack's father, a college professor, left his mother when Jack was five years old. He acknowledged that the only memory of his father and mother together was constant fighting.

At a young age Jack became his mother's sole emotional support. She made it clear to Jack that she was never going to get married again and that he was *her little man*. Jack had no other siblings and remembers spending many afternoons drinking tea and shopping with his mother, a perfectionist who would tell Jack how messy he was if he spilled two crumbs on their sparkling kitchen floor. If he brought home a B on his report card she'd berate him because it wasn't an A.

Jack learned how to make his mother happy. He'd tell her what she wanted to hear, giving her superficial compliments that always made her smile. "That's my little man," she'd say and kiss him on the cheek.

When Jack started playing baseball his mother would walk away from the game if he struck out. "Too humiliating," she'd tell him when he came home. Jack became the best player on the baseball team and obtained straight A's throughout his later school years. He gained admiration from teachers and students alike for his fine manners, good grades, and athletic ability. His mother always found something to criticize.

Jack said his father came to visit only five times while Jack was growing up.

Jack's Assessment:

Jack is looking for something he's not getting in his relationship with Megan, who's miserable with Jack most of the time. Without assigning blame, suffice it to say that these two are in a partnership that has broken down. One or both may decide they don't want to attend therapy—thereby basically walking away from a partnership system they see as faulty. Megan may not feel the broken system is worth fixing, and Jack may have decided he was done with the partnership system before he initiated his latest affair, with Vanessa.

Two people in a relationship will often do anything

they can to keep the relationship the same, this is called homeostasis. But whether by mistake or by accident, it may shift. Partners change and grow all the time. The relationship has to survive the bad as well as the good. Some people have such a difficult time dealing with the hardships of a relationship that they find a way to leave the partner, intentionally or not.

This is why communication is the primary component in any relationship that's going to last. Both partners should communicate their needs and desires, their strengths and their weaknesses.

Jack's Recommendations:

- Jack's insecurity issues should be assessed and addressed in therapy, which may be lengthy. A narcissist's low self-esteem is deeply rooted, and narcissists tend to see all their problems as caused by others.
- His childhood issues stemming from his mother's narcissistic personality need to be assessed and addressed in therapy. Jack should try to learn how to be empathetic toward other people's feelings and through therapy sessions. Because he may never be able to truly empathize with others, he needs to learn how to demonstrate a perceived empathy.
- He needs to address the reality that his actions often hurt others.
- His perception that only his feelings matter needs to be confronted.

- Group therapy would benefit Jack, as he would get feedback on his empathy from others in the group.
- Couples therapy with Megan is strongly advised if these two choose to stay in a committed relationship.

Tools: Are you a Narcissistic Cheater?

1. Do you see yourself as more important than others? Do you see yourself as "special?"
2. Are you constantly exaggerating your achievements? If you don't think so, have other people told you that you do this?
3. Do you see others as insignificant compared to you?
4. Are you preoccupied with ideal love?
5. Do you believe that only people of high status are worthy of your time and attention?
6. Do you feel you deserve only the best? Do you have a sense of entitlement? For example, do you only want to be seen with a beautiful woman? Only want the best table, the best seats?
7. Have you found that you require a lot of admiration?
8. Do you often take advantage of others to make sure you get what you want? For example, would you take advantage of your friend's beautiful/handsome spouse if their

marriage wasn't going well? Would you perceive a chance for an affair?

9. Have you found it difficult to experience empathy for your partner when you're in a committed relationship? No matter what you may say, do you really not care much?

10. Do you feel that everyone is envious of you and your partner because you seem to be special?

11. Is your attitude toward your partner often arrogant?

If you answered yes to five or more questions you may be a narcissistic cheater.

7 Tips for Dealing with the Narcissistic Personality Cheater (NPC)

1. When confronting a NPC, always start with a sincere compliment.

2. Be prepared for the NPC to use shallow and egocentric defenses, such as: "I had to cheat because I am such a sexual person, and you don't fulfill my needs," or "I cheated because he/she was so hot and was so into me."

3. Keep in mind that NPC's are over-compensating for deep-rooted insecurities with a haughty, confident persona.

4. Be aware that the NPC will typically lack the ego strength to deal with constructive criticism and is likely to react by projecting

jealous tendencies and personality issues of his/her own onto you.

5. Know that if you confront the NPC's infidelity overtly the reaction may be to blame you or become defensive. NPC's often think sexual norms don't apply to them. For this and other reasons the NPC may find it difficult or impossible to see your viewpoint on sexual issues. A therapist may need to intervene.

6. Most important: The NPC may need several years of therapy in order to effect positive change. The willingness to stick with the therapy is a good sign, but narcissism is among all disorders one of the hardest to treat in therapy.

7. When looking for a therapist, interview until you find one who works well with the NPC, otherwise the therapy will be short-lived.

4

NARCISSISTIC CHEATER
FEMALE

Lauren

"If we're going to do this, let's do it right," Lauren said. "He's the best, simply the best there is in bronze. You said you were going to make it for my birthday. Do you want a bronze of me in the entrance or not?"

"Sure, if that's what you want," David said. "But a hundred thousand dollars?"

"It'll look fabulous—and you promised me for my birthday!"

"Let's do that Nike replica," he said. "That's only ten thousand in marble."

"Now it's about the money? Don't be cheap, honey, it's supposed to be a gift.""Well I didn't know it was going to be a hundred thousand. That's way too much, even for custom bronze."

"But it's a Bernini! Only Spielberg has one." Lauren was pouting, which she thought made her look adorable. She was right. "This entry is our first impression—do you want to stand out or not?"

"Let's just think about it."

"Fine—while you're thinking, you won't be touching me," she said.

"Honey, don't flip out. You know I love you." David hadn't had sex for quite a while.

"Prove it. I want a Bernini bronze of me—there." She pointed to their gated courtyard entrance.

"Okay, okay. I give up. Get the contract, I'll sign."

She kissed him with the contract and pen in her hand. David signed and added 'Happy Birthday, Lauren' on the side of the page.

"How long does it take?"

"Nine months."

"When does he need the money?"

"Now. Up front."

"All of it?"

"It's custom art."

"Okay, okay. Get the checkbook, I'll move some cash from my product placement account."

She kissed him and handed him the checkbook. "Now do you know I love you?" he said.

"Yes." She giggled. "It wasn't clear to me for the past three years—until this moment."

"Take me to bed," he said. "I'll make it even more clear."

Sex meant Lauren putting on an expensive nightgown and strutting back and forth. Then she'd lie down and let him have oral sex with her. After that he could get on top and thrust in the missionary position for as long as he wanted—which wasn't all that long.

He would climax, she'd pretend she did. They'd hug, he'd fall asleep, then Lauren would get up and buy stuff on eBay.

On the plus side, Lauren was beautiful, an asset for the LA party scene, and instrumental in his getting a couple deals for his movie production company.

He liked her feisty personality, but living with Lauren was like living in a house of mirrors—figuratively and literally. Even in Hollywood he hadn't run into someone who enjoyed looking at herself so much. She was also changeable, often difficult, and always a severe strain on his wallet.

"David, you were invited to Sol's birthday party at Bel-Air Country Club," she said the next day. "I wasn't invited."

"It's a guy golf thing," he said.

"No, it's not. Chicky is going."

"Well, it must have been an oversight," he said. "I'll ask for you. Lauren.

Something awful happened yesterday, I forgot to tell you."

"What?"

"You know Ezra Berman?"

"I don't remember him."

"Sure you do, he's been my sound guy for fifteen years. You talked to his wife Barbara at the last wrap party. Anyway, Ezra had a heart attack and died yesterday on the set. Only forty-two, and they have two small children. I'd like to do something nice for his family."

"I'm sure he's got insurance," she said.

"He's been a very loyal employee." Lauren peered into the mirror, looking for crows' feet or any sign she might need a Botox injection.

"What did you say, honey? I've got my make-up gal coming in a minute and I didn't hear you."

"Never mind. I'll take care of it," David said.

"Have a good day at work."

"Bye." David passed Wendy, Lauren's make-up artist, on his way out.

"Hi, Wendy."

"Hi, David."

"Wendy, how much better does my wife look when you do her make-up versus when she does it herself?"

"About one percent—she knows how to do her own make-up."

"That's what I thought," David said. "How much do I pay you to come here?"

"I charge half price for you because I come so often. About five hundred for a house call."

"Thanks, Wendy. I just wondered."

Lauren opened the door. "Wendy, I need you so bad today. Come in, come in."

Lauren looked perfect by the time Wendy was done with her.

"I can't wait to meet the duke, are we on time?"

"Yeah, we can make it," said Wendy. "He's in Beverly Hills too."

"How did his wife die?"

"Not sure. She was sick a long time."

"What did you tell him about me?"

"I told him you had exquisite taste and you'd offer your opinion on what his decorator's doing to the place. I think he misses having a second voice in the house."

They were in Wendy's new Porsche heading east on Sunset Blvd, their hair blowing in the wind. Lauren felt younger and freer with Wendy. She was a smart, sharp twenty-five-year-old who'd do well in this town.

They pulled into a Beverly Hills mansion.

"Oh, I like this so much better than our house," Lauren said. "I wish we had a longer drive—and that's beautiful landscaping."

"Remember, he's not really a duke, people just call him that." They rang the bell. Even the doorbell had beautiful tones. A servant led them to a striking man in a library.

"Duke Farhar, this is Lauren Gold."

"Hello, Duke."

"Lauren, a pleasure to meet you."

Lauren was dressed in a pink strapless sundress and expensive high heels with a sexy pink ruffle on them. She looked stunning. Duke obviously liked what he saw.

He was handsome, an aristocrat so far as Lauren was concerned, and one of the richest men in the world. His Beverly Hills home was a palace and the renovation was extensive.

"Wendy," Duke said, "you'll find Lilly in the living room waiting for you."

"Okay."

"May I take you on a tour of the renovation, Lauren?"

"Yes, I'd love that."

Lauren wanted this man and his power right away. Duke wanted her when she started sharing ideas with her special flair. She thought the living room needed more warmth and told him he should put in more mirrors.

"People like to walk by mirrors. It's just a human thing," she said.

Within days Duke and Lauren were having an affair. Though Duke had twelve bedrooms to choose from, she insisted they go out of town where she wouldn't be known. Wherever they went, Duke made sure Lauren's little behind was sitting on plush suede or leather. Duke hired helicopters and paid for plane tickets. Sometimes they drove to Palm Springs or flew to San Francisco, Las Vegas, or Santa Barbara. It was an exciting time, and Lauren loved being swept off her feet.

When he started needing her opinion in the evenings, David began to get suspicious. By the time the rumors confirmed his suspicions, Lauren told him she was moving out and filing for a divorce.

David was served divorce papers the same day the bronze statue of Lauren was installed in his entry. But Lauren had proof on the contract that it was a birthday present. She had the key to the gate, and when David went to work the next day, she had movers bring the large bronze over to Duke's garden.

Lauren and Duke married the weekend after her divorce was final. They were happy for several years, until Duke lost his fortune in bad investments. Lauren lost interest.

She did feel sorry for him—for a moment. Then she left him for a Disney Executive.

She took with her everything she'd acquired from David, part of Duke's assets and half of his remaining investments, several mirrors, and her bronze Bernini statue.

Lauren's Meeting:

Lauren walked into my office dressed head to toe in designer clothes. She usually sees a therapist in California, but she'd been at the Mayo Clinic in Rochester for severe migraines. Her husband demanded she see some of the best neurologists in the country.

"Idiots, every one of them. They can't find anything wrong. They say it's stress related and I need to see you. Please. I've tried all the medications and every relaxation technique out there. What can you do for me?"

"Biofeedback and visualization techniques often work for migraines," I said. Often a self-absorbed person exhibits psychosomatic symptoms to avoid what's really bothering them mentally or psychologically.

"I'll try anything," she said.

Lauren's Background:

Lauren grew up in Chicago, where her father made a comfortable living in the computer industry until he was laid off from his job due to depression and anxiety. He tried to commit suicide by ingesting pills. Lauren's mother found him unconscious and called 911. Lauren claimed he had to go to the psychiatric unit for several months, and her mother was hugely embarrassed.

Lauren's parents divorced when she was six and her sister eight. According to Lauren, her mother remarried the president of one of the biggest financial firms in the state. Lauren said the happiest day of her life was when she was a flower girl in her mom's picturesque wedding.

She said she'd seen her father several times after the divorce but didn't feel comfortable around him. By age ten, she asked that he not contact her. "My stepfather met all our needs—he bought us anything we wanted."

Lauren's Assessment:

In Lauren's eyes, nothing is more important than money. Since she lacks empathy, once the money is gone, so is she. Lauren is definitely not a for-better-or-worse kind of woman.

At this point Lauren feels she needs money and a powerful man to get the love she wants and needs. She mistakes superficial social connections with true friendship. She perceives the gifts her husband buys her as true affection—the bigger the gift, the more her husband must adore and love her.

Lauren comes off as vain, self-sufficient, superficial, and self-righteous. She seems to lack any awareness of her own emptiness or that she's incomplete as a person. Her doubts come out in various ways, including hypochondriac preoccupations.

According to Lauren's medical records, in the past two years she's complained of three neurological problems, two gastrointestinal issues, and three sexual issues. The doctors were unable to find anything wrong. She denies any psychological issues. But she takes Xanax to relax on really hectic days and Ambien to sleep.

Lauren's Recommendations:

- Lauren should try biofeedback for her migraine headaches.
- She would benefit from group therapy so she can observe how she affects other people.
- She would benefit from individual therapy in which she addresses her family life.
- She needs to find the psychological source of her "medical" issues.
- She should be assessed for depression and anxiety.
- She would benefit from couples therapy with her current husband.
- Her medication needs to be assessed, as it may not be appropriate for her current mental status.
- She would benefit from several years of psychotherapy to establish empathy and care for others.
- She needs to address her low self-esteem issues, which drive her toward monetary things as opposed to self-love.

Tools: Are You a Narcissistic Cheater?

1. Do you feel your mate isn't worthy of your company? Have you found that there are very few people worthy of your company?
2. Do you often find you need the best of everything? Do you feel you deserve it?
3. Are your emotions often shallow? Give some thought to this and try to be honest.
4. Do you think you have few friends because everyone is envious of your accomplishments?
5. Are you always right and your partner always wrong?
6. Do you find that you have grandiose thoughts?
7. Do you get frustrated because your mate isn't as smart as you?
8. Do you like to be seen with the most successful person in the room?
9. Have you found it hard to discover a partner who even holds a candle to you?

If you answered yes to four or more of these questions you may be a Narcissistic Cheater.

5

PATHOLOGICAL CHEATER
FEMALE

Danielle

"I'm in a Maui Art Gallery, not that it's any of Jasper's business."

"Danielle, come home. Lacy needs you, and Jasper's worried."

"There's nothing in Wichita that needs me, Mom. Hell, there's nothing in Wichita at all."

"At least talk to him," her mother said. "He's your husband and he loves you more than God loves the earth."

"Well, I don't care. I won't come back until I'm good and ready." Danielle's eyes widened as she spied her target. "Gotta go, Mom. Later."

She unbuttoned three buttons on her sheer Versace blouse, slipped on a high heel that had been dangling from a toe, and straightened her tight black skirt.

A man in an expensive Italian suit cruised the tourist trap art gallery, stopping at every painting for a couple of minutes.

"My name is Danielle," she said. "May I help you?"

He wore an expensive watch and tasteful diamond rings, and she guessed his fashionable tan came from sunning on private yachts.

"I'm Richard." He didn't turn. "I need nothing."

She had to make eye contact. She touched his right arm and stepped close to his side. He looked down at her. Her blouse was sheer and her bra was trimmed with lace. He took a step back.

"Forgive my rudeness," he said. "I'm Richard Polo."

"You looked a bit preoccupied, Richard, forgive me for interrupting you."

"You're not interrupting at all. You're a breath of fresh air."

"Would you like me to give you a tour of our gallery?"

"I'd love that," he said. The phone rang. "Do you need to get that?"

She looked at him from under lowered lashes.

"No, Richard, this time is just for you. They'll call back."

Several times on the gallery tour, Danielle would touch his arm gently or brush against him. Richard spent most of the time inhaling her scent.

"Where are you staying?" she asked.

"The Ritz," he said. "Would you like to have lunch today?"

"That would be lovely," she said.

"I should probably tell you I'm married," Richard said.

"So am I."

Danielle stepped in the back room to tell another employee she was leaving for the afternoon.

"You just started," the framer said. "You're supposed to be working out front all day."

But Danielle was already gone.

Over a long lunch she learned Richard had been married for thirty-five years and had four children. He was an exporter who owned glass shops in several cities and lived in Milan. He was very close to both his parents and had recently lost them in an auto accident.

It was obvious he was grieving, and all Danielle had to do was act sympathetic. Richard was touched.

"Are you paid on commission?" he asked.

"Yes," she said.

Richard had to take a call, and Danielle excused herself to visit the bathroom. Once there, she grabbed her cell phone and hit her speed dial.

"Hey, Owen, it's Danielle."

"Hey, lover,"

"What are you doing?"

"I shouldn't tell you." He sounded sad.

"Tell me, I'm here for you."

"I was just at my wife's grave," he said. "I really miss having a woman around. It's been almost a year. When are you going to come and meet me?"

"Soon. I'm on the road right now on a writing assignment and one of these days I'm going to surprise you."

"Promise?"

"Yes, I promise, lover."

"Are you going to send me another picture of you?" he asked.

"I had some taken by a professional photographer.

He took a lot of nudes—tasteful, you know. But he won't give me the photos until I pay him twelve hundred, and I don't have it." She started to cry.

"I could PayPal you the twelve hundred. Is that enough, do you need more?"

"If I had another five hundred I could make my rent too," she said.

"Okay, honey, I'll PayPal you the two thou. Can't wait to see your pictures."

"I'll send them as soon as I get them. Love you, Owen," she said.

"I love you too, honey. But come and meet me."

"I will. Soon," she said.

She looked at her missed calls. Another widower from Cincinnati. He wasn't close to any kind of pay-off and she wasn't in the mood. She'd call him later. She checked herself in the mirror. That shirt was worth every penny.

Her phone rang again.

"This is Brenda Vassar. We met at the woman's group on Wednesday. I'm the attorney who said I'd help you."

"Yes?" Danielle said.

"Well, I want to help—believe me, I know what sons-of-bitches men can be. If you're in an abusive relationship, you need to get out." Brenda sounded strong and confident.

"I can't. I just can't." Danielle kept her response slow, her voice timid.

"Why, what's holding you back?"

"I need money to leave and get my children here.

When I'm here, I feel like I can be who I truly am. I know now I'm not into men," she said. "I just want to find a lover who'll be good to me. A lover who won't hurt me again."

"I could be that lover," Brenda said.

"That's what scares me, Brenda. I'm so attracted to you—I've been attracted to women, but never like this. I think if we were together, we'd just explode."

"I want that explosion."

"How do you feel about kids?" Danielle asked.

"Love them," she said.

"You sure? Some people say that but they don't mean it."

"I mean it. I would take care of you."

"You don't really know me, Brenda."

"I know you enough to know I'd do my best to make it work."

"I have to go now," Danielle said. "Let's get together later."

She returned to Richard, got what she wanted from him, and met Brenda as planned.

"I'll never hurt you," Brenda said. "Let me take care of you."

"I can't stop thinking about the way you kissed me when we met after work," Danielle said. "I want you so bad."

"I want you too," Brenda said. "Let's get together tonight."

"I can't. I'm working. And I won't jump into a relationship without sending for my kids. My kids need me.

You'll have to be patient. It'll probably take me about a year to save enough money."

"I can't wait that long. How much do you need?"

"I need to pay off a five-thousand-dollar debt, then have money for the move. Ten thousand would probably cover it," she said.

"I'll get it for you tomorrow morning."

"If you PayPal me the money I can buy a ticket right away, fly to the mainland for the kids, and come right back. I could be back and settled by the end of the week. I'll get a sitter and we can go out this weekend."

"Where do I send it? I'll PayPal you now."

Danielle gave her the information, made a date with her for Sunday evening, and left to make her late date with Richard.

After dinner they went up to Richard's suite.

"I have nothing to offer you," he said.

"I want nothing from you, Richard." They kissed.

"I've been dying to see your clothes off since I met you," he said.

She obliged him and stripped, then turned slowly so he could take in her youthful body.

"Slower," he said.

She slowed and did everything he asked. When they were done having sex, she aroused him yet again. Afterwards he fell into a deep sleep. Danielle dressed, picked up her purse, and slid his credit cards out of his wallet. She hailed a cab, went to her motel room, changed her clothes, and put on a short dark wig. She grabbed her luggage and was on her way to the airport. As she waited for her flight, she went on line and charged a number of expensive items to Richard's credit cards, then flew to Honolulu under an alias.

Back home in Wichita, Jasper paced and poured his heart out to his mother-in-law.

"Why doesn't she come back to me?" he said. "Danielle knows I love her. I know she loves me. She married me, didn't she? She knows I'll get her anything I can."

"I don't know, honey," his mother-in-law said. "I just don't understand her."

"What about Lacey? Doesn't she care about Lacey?" Jasper looked exhausted as he rocked his eighteen-month-old daughter.

"Daddy loves you, Lacey. Don't worry. Daddy loves you. Mommy will come home."

Danielle's Meeting:

What Danielle was not aware of was the fact that Richard's brother, Hunter, was an FBI agent who made some calls to a few of his buddies. April 9th, 2007 Danielle was picked up in St Paul, Minnesota, she was meeting a prominent government official for dinner at the St. Paul Grill Hotel.

As soon as she walked up to the desk to get the key that was left for her, the St. Paul police greeted her. Danielle ended up at the *Minnesota* Correctional Facility-*Shakopee, a woman's prison in Shakopee, Minnesota* for two years.

As I walked into the woman's prison that day, it didn't feel like I was walking into a correctional facility. There wasn't a fence like most facilities, and the yard was absent of any officers to guard.

The minute I walked into the facility, however, I was reminded that it was high security. An officer checked my bag and I walked through several steel doors that locked loudly behind me.

I walked straight to the segregation unit and asked to see Danielle in the interview room.

"So, Danielle, are you ready to get out of here and back in your cell?" I asked.

"Hell, no, if that bitch touches me again, I swear I will kill her with my bare hands," she grimaced.

"You don't want to have to stay in the segregation unit until you get out of here," I said.

"I'm just fine here, Dr. Wood. I haven't been lonely since I arrived. Do you want to know something? All the men I was writing to before, all the lonely and widowed men, are still writing me and sending me more money than ever," she said.

"My husband writes me every day and sends pictures of the kid. How sad it that? I even found a website where men log on and talk to woman in prison. There is also a lesbian site for chicks in prison. I already have five men and three woman who think they are in love with me," she admitted.

"Danielle try to get out in the yard for some exercise today, it's a really nice day out and it would do you good to think about other things than how to manipulate people once in a while," I suggested.

"Whatever you say, doc. Hey can I get some Trazodone?" Danielle asked in her sweetest voice, "I have had the hardest time sleeping."

"We don't give offenders Trazodone anymore as it gets too expensive."

"You could make an exception for me, couldn't you, doc?"

"Have a good day Danielle. I will check on you tomorrow. Good bye."

"Let's talk more about that Trazodone tomorrow," she yelled as I walked out the door."

Danielle's Background:

Danielle was trained to con. Her mother was a petty thief who stole from discount retail stores. She often used her children as a distraction. When they were infants, she stuffed jewelry from Wal-Mart in their strollers. Danielle says she remembers these thefts going back to when she was three or four years old. She thought of it as getting free prizes. When she was fourteen, she and her mother were caught and booked with petty theft.

A search of their home led the police to other stolen merchandise, and her mother was sent away. Danielle was left in the care of an aunt she hated and ran to the arms of boys who found her 'hot'. She soon became sexually active in exchange for gifts—a cell phone, a TV set, or a stereo became her bounty for small sexual favors. Once she was practiced she wanted a bigger pond and left Nebraska for richer targets.

Danielle's Assessment:

When Danielle had an unplanned pregnancy, she married the child's father. Danielle and her high school boyfriend Jasper went through the motions of settling down. Even a nice house paid in full by Jasper's wealthy family wasn't enough to keep Danielle in Wichita. She has serious personality flaws and isn't capable of settling down. She does not feel empathy for others around her, including her child, husband, and family.

Danielle's scams will soon catch up with her and eventually she'll have a lot of time to think in prison. But Richard won't want the publicity, nor will Brenda, the attorney who feels foolish for her stupid purchase of a relationship. The widowers won't either with their embarrassment over being taken by a con artist.

Meanwhile, Jasper has no idea what Danielle is doing. Danielle feels superior to those around her, to the point that no one else matters. She has no interest in her marriage with Jasper. She did not bond with her child, nor will she. Jasper should get out of the marriage, but if Danielle at some point should become aware that her life is empty of everything that would make it truly satisfying, she might seek therapy.

Danielle's Recommendations:

- Danielle needs an assessment to diagnosis her personality disorder and psychopathic tendencies.

- Danielle needs an empathy course to teach her how to respond to others.
- Group therapy would help her understand how her behavior and personality style affect others.
- Individual therapy can help her explore why she has problems bonding to her daughter and her husband and learn how to express her true feeling verbally.
- A class on ethics and values would help Danielle learn from her previous mistakes.

Tools: Are You a Pathological Cheater?

1. Do you find yourself often manipulating, lying, or conning your partner? Friends? Acquaintances?
2. Do you have little to no empathy for your partner's feelings?
3. Do you feel an adrenaline rush when taking advantage of others?
4. Do your feelings and needs come before everyone else's?
5. Do you break rules? What about laws? Do you fail to conform to what society would consider normal?
6. Have you found you disregard safety for yourself and your partner?
7. Do you lack remorse if you mistreat, steal from, or cheat on your partner?

8. Do you have problems with impulsive behavior around your partner?
9. Does your partner, due to fighting or verbal abuse, say you're aggressive?
10. Do you lie to others for your own profit or gain?

If you answered yes to four or more of the questions above, you may be a Pathological Cheater.

6

CHARISMATIC CHEATER
MALE

Mike

"No, thank you," Ann said to the pesky man in the bar.

"Why can't I just buy you one drink? You must know someone who needs a used car—I can get any kind."

"Please," Ann said, "I don't want to make a scene, just leave me alone."

"Hi, baby," a strong, handsome stranger said. Ann felt a man's hand around her waist. He gave her a tingling kiss on the cheek.

"Sorry I was late but I had to take your mother to the bank and drop the kids off at the babysitter's."

"No problem," she said. "I believe this gentleman was just leaving."

The man who was trying to buy Ann a drink went over to a group of guys in the corner. She saw money being exchanged.

"Must have been a bet," said the tall, blond man. He turned to go.

"Wait," Ann said. "I want to thank you."

"No problem," he said, "I like to help a damsel in distress."

Ann could still feel his arm on her waist and his kiss on her cheek.

"What's your name?" she asked.

"Mike." He turned away. "Can I buy you a drink—for saving me?"

"No thanks, I don't drink," Mike said.

"A Coke?"

"I don't do caffeine, either."

"A Sprite?"

"Your name is?"

"Ann."

"Ann, I'm glad I could help you out of a jam, but I really have to go."

"Hey, Slapshot!" A perky, beautiful girl grabbed Mike from behind. "I've been waiting for you all day."

Mike leaned over and kissed the girl on top of her head. She beamed up at Mike, then looked over at Ann.

"Oh, I'm sorry." The girl stuck out her hand. "Are you one of Mike's hockey groupies? I have to fight them off all the time."

"No, this is Ann," Mike said. "I just saved her from a horrible fate." He shook her hand. "It was nice to meet you."

Ann was surprised to feel a piece of paper in her hand. As she walked out the door she looked at it: Mike's cell number.

For some reason she couldn't get Mike off her mind. She

watched a couple of hockey games on television, awed by Mike's athletic ability. Finally, she called him.

"Mike, this is Ann—from the bar a couple of weeks ago."

"Sorry," he said. "I don't know of any Ann from the bar. I have to go."

"Wait," Ann said. "I was the damsel in distress. You kissed me on the cheek and pretended you knew me so the guy would leave me alone."

"Sure, I remember you now. Are you still trying to buy me a Sprite? Because I heard the Sprite is really good at the Four Seasons. Meet me there at eight o'clock tonight."

Ann walked around her apartment over the next three hours, too restless to sit. She started looking through her closet. By the time she was putting on the little black dress, she knew she was going. She was a good-looking girl; she could have anyone she wanted. What was it about Mike? She'd never had to work so hard for a man before.

Was it because Mike was in demand? Was it because he was near super stardom and she wanted a small part of him? Because he was gorgeous and charming and well heeled? Didn't matter—she couldn't wait to see him.

Ann drove to the hotel. Mike had left a key with the concierge desk and was waiting for her in his room. He met her with a kiss and extravagant compliments about how gorgeous she looked. He'd ordered a bottle of

Cristal champagne and chocolate-covered strawberries. They talked for several hours about Mike's career.

When he asked her a few questions about herself she answered but felt lightheaded. She felt his hand slide up her skirt and did nothing to stop him.

At one point Ann asked, "What about Amanda?"

"What about Amanda?"

Ann and Mike had ravenous, animalistic sex. Afterwards, Mike held Ann for a long time, told her how great she felt, how much he wanted to see her again. Ann left on cloud nine. Mike continued to call, and they saw each other once a week. Mike said he'd love to see her more but that was all he could fit in with his busy hockey schedule.

Ann asked about Amanda again. Mike said Amanda had left him because she found out Mike was cheating on her.

"The really hot girls don't put up with a man cheating on them," he said. Ann felt her stomach drop when he said that. Nevertheless, Ann thought she was different. She couldn't get enough of Mike and she hoped one day he'd propose.

Ann became Mike's new girlfriend. Admirers surrounded him at every party and every function, and there were so many gorgeous women everywhere that Ann felt like she was constantly defending her territory, like she was always vying for Mike's attention. She started feeling jealous and resentful.

One evening after a game, Ann walked up to the locker room to see Mike standing against the wall, talking to a

Delta flight attendant. Just as Ann approached, she saw Mike give the woman his number.

He grabbed Ann by the arm and kissed her cheek. "This is my lovely girlfriend, Ann," he said.

Mike's Meeting:

It was a bright spring day outside the Minnesota Department of Corrections, but inside the corridors were dimly lit and covered in dismal gray paint.

Officer Perry answered my knock right away.

"I'll get him for you, doc. It's sad, Mike was my favorite player. This could mean our whole season is ruined—and for him it could be years."

Officer Perry left the room and came back with a tall, blond, handsome young man dressed in the standard orange prison jumpsuit.

"Please sit, Mike." I looked at his intake sheet from the nursing department and his charge paper from the police. "I see this is your first visit here."

"Doctor, this was a mistake," he said. "You have to help me get me out of this place. I don't belong here."

I continued to study the new entries in his file. Mike demonstrated excessive emotionality and attention-seeking behavior, not odd for a pro sports player.

"Hey," he said, his voice dropping to a whisper. "I play hockey, right? So I have all these people who want to be around me. They want to touch me, stare at me, get my autograph, you know, that type of thing, right?" He leaned in close to me.

All during the visit, Mike leaned into my personal space, demonstrating apparent openness combined with a bit of flirtation. He demanded to be the center of attention even though most offenders in the intake unit didn't know who he was. I saw him glance out of the corner of his eye at a female officer who walked by. Mike's emotional expression seemed shallow and shifted rapidly.

"Hey, sit back!" Officer Perry yelled at one point. "Keep your distance from the doctor." Mike moved his chair back a little.

"Anyway, like I was saying, everyone wants a part of me. So I met this Delta flight attendant, Jamie. I assumed she was single; she was out with her girlfriends when we met. So I took her to my hotel room and went for it. I had no idea she was married.

"Anyway, so we were done two weeks ago, but her husband found out about me. He called me from her cell and I answered. He ranted and I hung up on him. Then he waited for me after a game. He ran down the arena corridor screaming at me, 'You son of a bitch, you're fucking my wife!'

"I could see he was a little business guy or something, but he raised his arms and I wasn't sure if he had a weapon, so I checked him against the wall like he was trying to score a goal on me. For most players it would have been no big deal. Anyone on the rink takes fifty checks against the wall in every game—just like that. I have sixty pounds and more muscle, so when I shoved him, he went flying and hit his head on the wood.

"I went home thinking the guy's going to be okay, but he hasn't come around yet. It wasn't my fault—I reacted with my instincts. He came after me, right, Doctor?"

His speech was impressionistic, lacked detail.

"The next thing I know, there's a knock on my door. It was the police and they've kept me up all night asking me questions.

"I have to get out of here now. I have a game this week. Team management lawyers will smooth everything over for me."

He slid his hand through his hair and said, "I hate my mug shot. It doesn't even look like me and now it's everywhere—TMZ, People, all the news."

Mike's Background:

Mike always excelled in sports. The older of two boys, he was competing with his little brother when he was still in diapers. As they became older, Mike won all the sporting events.

Tired of being in Mike's shadow, his brother quit competing in sports and Mike received all the accolades for his athletic gifts. Mike was president of his senior class and voted most popular student in school. He was captain of the hockey team the year he led his team his team to victory National Hockey Night with the winning goal, which made him an instant Canadian celebrity.

By the time he was signed to play pro hockey, he had his own entourage of groupies. Women were always drawn to Mike and he took advantage of his celebrity, usually knowing he'd never be calling the women back.

Mike decided not to settle for average women but to go after other public personalities such as, models, anchorwomen, journalists, etc. Still, if a girl was extraordinary or caught his eye in some way he'd let her in for a short time before moving on to greener grass.

Mike's Assessment:

Mike has several characteristics of a charismatic cheater. He has achieved celebrity status in his athletic field and uses it to his advantage. He doesn't feel he has to put the energy into his relationships that most people do. He told me women are never a priority—they're like buses, another will come along any minute.

Mike has been in hockey skates since he was three years old. He grew up in Canada and hockey was his life. "I'm more comfortable when I have skates on my feet," he told me. "Since I spent hours on the ice every day, I've bonded closer to the guys that watch my back.

"Chicks are great—they're the icing on the cake. But growing up I spent most of my time with Dad and my brothers on the ice, never saw my mom or sister that much. And I'd rather scout girls in a bar with my buddies than go out and spend an evening with a girl. I've never gone home alone when I just wait around. Sooner or later that bus comes along.

"I'm known for my butch hockey ability and women go down easy for me. All I do is tell them what they want to hear. Any other guy in my shoes would do the same thing, you know?"

Mike's Recommendations:

- Mike's braggadocio masks a deep-seated emotional void and insecurities that need to be explored and addressed in individual therapy.
- He has the best chance of success with a female therapist.
- Mike needs to be assessed for his violence and anger management.
- He would benefit from group therapy to see how his interactions affect other people. Mike needs to learn how to feel empathy for his victim and his family with a special emphasis on learning genuine empathy for women in general.
- Mike needs years of psychoanalytic therapy to work on his core issues revolving around the narcissistic self. The psychoanalytic therapist could help Mike use transference and counter transference issues with a love for self-object that may eventually allow him to respect others.

Tools: Are You a Charismatic Cheater?

1. Are you a celebrity, or perceived as one? Even if you're the champ of your company's tennis team, that counts.
2. Are you uncomfortable in situations where you're not the focus of attention? Do you find yourself constantly seeking attention?

3. Do most of your interactions with the opposite sex include flirting, or seductive or provocative behavior?
4. Do you find yourself demonstrating rapid but shallow emotional involvement from one partner to another to suit your present needs?
5. At times, do you tend to exaggerate your feelings for your partners, telling them how much you care for them even if it's not true?
6. Do you have a style of speech that sounds impressive, yet lacks depth or detail?
7. Do you find yourself using charm and story-telling skills to get what you want in life?

If you answered yes to five or more of the questions above you may be a charismatic cheater.

7

CHARISMATIC CHEATER
FEMALE

Ava

"Ava always gets the front," Stacy said. "Everyone knows those tables get the best tips."

"George likes her. She's down to working Thursday, Friday, and Saturday now—and she works a six-hour shift instead of eight," Lilly said.

"It's not fair. I've been here five years, she came three months ago," Stacy said.

"Careful—if you say anything, it could get worse."

"I know. I'm not going to, but it's just not fair. What's she got that I don't?"

"Shhh, here she comes."

Ava walked to her locker and started to change into her cocktail waitress costume.

She had a young Heather Locklear look: piercing deep blue eyes, platinum blond hair, and a professional tan to set off an incredible smile and one of the best bodies in Minnesota.

"Wow, Ava, nice heels! Where'd you get those?"

"Those are Christian Louboutins, aren't they?"

"Right," Ava said.

"Did you get them on eBay used or something?"

"They're new—a gift."

"Your husband?"

She shut her locker and turned to them. "They're just shoes."

She had on a strapless cocktail dress with a bustier that made incredible cleavage on her petite leggy frame.

"We better punch in or we'll be late," Stacy said. The girls walked out together, passing by their manager, George, who checked their appearance before going on the floor.

"Ava, can I see you a minute?" George asked.

"Sure you can." Ava dropped into a soft Marilyn Monroe voice whenever she talked to men.

"Ava, you look extra gorgeous tonight," he said. "Nice shoes."

"Thanks."

"I'd love to see them next to my bed," he said.

"What would your wife say?"

"Well, she can't say anything if I put her on a cruise for a few months," he said.

"George, I think the sex would be so good we wouldn't come into work and the casino would fall apart without you, so we better not."

He giggled like a schoolboy. He just couldn't take his eyes off her.

"Anyone special tonight, George?"

"Yes, walk with me. On table four you'll see two cowboy hats, one gray, one black. The guy in the black hat is Jack Brown, a Texas Hold'em runner-up. The gray hat is his buddy Lloyd. Jack's worth a lot, so let's keep him happy."

"Will do, George."

"Table six, there's another guy in a silk shirt with flames on it. Johnny Tiger, he's a NASCAR guy with bucks. Table eight there's a guy with glasses, looks like an accountant, playing blackjack—he's low-key but he's a Cargill. I'll introduce you to Jack Brown."

"Thanks for the tip, George. I'll keep them happy," Ava said. They walked across the casino to the bigger stakes tables.

"We aren't going to see your husband tonight, are we?"

"He's playing softball and going out with his friends after. He knows not to come here," she said.

They stood before a blackjack table. Two cowboy hats sat in the three and four positions.

"Jack and Lloyd, this is Ava. She'll make sure you get anything you need," George said.

Jack and Lloyd drank in Ava's looks.

"George, I believe what I need is her," Jack said. "What a filly. You're beautiful, darlin'."

"Thank you." Ava looked deeply into his eyes and smiled. "Can I get you anything to drink?"

"Pinch's straight up."

"Jack Daniels iced."

"I'll be right back."

Ava flirted through a couple of rounds with her special customers. She'd made almost $500 within two hours. It was definitely a good night—until Scott came in.

Nobody noticed him at first. He stood and watched Ava serving the blackjack tables, watched her flirting with two men in cowboy hats. Drunk from several beers after his softball game, he charged over to the table.

"You should come home right now. Damn it, Ava, you've got to quit this job—"

"Bounce softball player by table four," came through the headphones. In seconds two bouncers had dragged Scott out.

"Is he yours, Ava?" Jack asked.

"He's a customer here," she said. "He just thinks he's married to me. Need another drink, guys?"

George and Lloyd had dropped a lot of money on the tables and decided to go back to their rooms for a while to party.

"Ava," Jack said, "we have friends joining us at midnight. I wonder if you'd do me a favor. Grab a bottle of Pinch's and Jack Daniels and come to Room 1655."

"Sure, Jack."

She told George she was leaving the floor, got the bottles, and knocked on the door to room 1655.

"Come on in. You can set the bottles on the bar, then we need to have a talk."

"Sure, but I have to get back to the floor soon."

"George won't mind. I'll tell him you helped me."

"What do you need?"

"Lloyd already ordered the girls for tonight, I'm just a curious guy. You're so beautiful, I need to know something."

"What?" Ava was a little scared but knew she could handle most situations.

"Like I said, I'm a curious guy, and I just got to see you naked."

"Oh, sorry, I don't do that. We aren't allowed to do that."

"I don't take no for an answer."

"I'm married. That upset guy downstairs was my husband, Scott."

"I figured. Well, one day you may leave him, Ava, and you'll need a nest egg. I'll tip you big if you undress for me."

"Sorry, no. I don't do that."

Jack laughed. "You're a terrific negotiator, Ava. But it's a bluff. You have a tell, and I'll win this round."

Thirty minutes later Ava left the room, hyperventilating. She'd earned $5,000 in cash for a three-minute partial strip, no sex, no touch, just down to her stockings and shoes. The exhibitionist in her found it thrilling.

Back at the front tables she picked up a $5 tip and only a $10 tip from the Cargill guy. She found herself wanting another experience like the one with Jack.

Jack and Lloyd never let on about Ava, but they did leave glowing remarks about her on their comment card. Her salary was raised, and each weekend George made sure she was assigned to special customers. Sometimes Scott sat outside in his 4 x 4 when Ava was working, unable to come into the casino. He watched to make sure she didn't come out with anyone. She didn't. He thought she'd been having affairs—she seemed secretive and distant. She had lots more of those fancy shoes and expensive clothes. Way out of his league for what he brought home from his construction job and what she made at the casino.

She said she wasn't having an affair and that Scott had to trust her. She said she loved him. After tailing her for a week, Scott decided she must have been telling the truth.

Meeting:

When Ava came into the first therapy session with her husband at 5:00 in the afternoon, she was dressed in a little sundress with high stiletto heels and Scott was in work clothes.

"So what brings you here?" I asked.

"Well, Denise—may I call you Denise?" Ava said with a huge smile. "Dr. Wood sounds stuffy and I feel like I know you already."

I wore a new blazer. She seemed to be fixating on the buttons. Then tears welled up in her big blue eyes.

"Scott thinks I'm cheating on him—he was following me, and I don't like that. I feel like he doesn't trust me. I feel violated." Ava sobbed into her hands. "I can't be married to a man who doesn't trust me. What can I do?" When she looked up, I saw no tears. Her makeup was still perfect.

Scott tried to put his arms around her.

"Get your hands off me!" she yelled.

"I didn't trust her for a while," Scott said. "I followed her for a week and she was just going to work and coming home. I told her I was sorry." He turned to Ava. "I swear I'll never do that to you again. It's just that you're so beautiful and every man wants you. I can't help it, I get so jealous sometimes."

Ava stopped crying and looked up at him.

"Really? You'll never do it again?"

"Never."

"Denise, sorry we wasted your time. Who decorated your office? Love the colors! I bet it was you. I can tell by looking at you, you're a really classy woman. We should go shopping sometime."

"Ethically, I can't see my clients out of the office," I said.

"Oh, too bad. You seem like you'd be great fun," she said. Then she slipped her arms around Scott's neck. "You silly, how could you ever think I'd cheat on you?" This in her sweetest voice as she cuddled up to him. They stood up to leave.

"I love you so damn much, Ava."

"Ava and Scott, since you're here, why don't you sit back down and we can finish our session," I said.

"Oh, I guess, sure," Ava said. "If you think we need to, okay. I don't want you to get the wrong idea about us, Denise."

The young couple sat down and came for many more sessions.

Ava's Background:

Ava's style of speech was animated but skimpy when it came to details. She told me that when she was growing up her mother was a stripper, had "a lot of sex" in the apartment where they lived, and "may" have been a prostitute on the side. Ava was the youngest of six children, none of them from the same father. "I was the one who was always in trouble," she said. She drank alcohol and smoked cigarettes regularly when she was ten and was having sex with older boys by fourteen. According to Ava, her mother knew about it but didn't care. Ava said her mother only cared about her brothers.

Ava's Assessment:

Ava's dress, hair, and makeup tend to be provocative or seductive, even in inappropriate situations. This gets her the attention she needs, but her own attention tends to be shallow, lack any true emotion, and shift rapidly.

Ava presents herself as lively and dramatic, but she's concerned to the point of obsession over what others think of her and spends a disproportionate amount of money, time, and energy on designer clothes and grooming. She feels uncomfortable if she isn't the center of all the attention. She likes to think of herself as the life of the party. Therefore, she makes sure she's the big hit with pleasing male clients, at all costs. Ava charms all the new men that come into the club with her open flirtations.

She spoke about how wonderful her boss was yet couldn't articulate why she felt this way. I noticed that her emotions were like a roller coaster—one moment she'd be crying inconsolably, the next she'd be laughing about something she found "hilarious." Often neither the tears nor the laughter seemed to come from any place beneath the surface she presents to the world—her emotions don't seem real, and I doubt that Ava feels very real to herself.

Ava's Recommendations:

- Ava needs individual therapy to work through her childhood issues. This will enable her to explore with the therapist who she really is so that she can develop her own personality—not just a persona.
- Therapy can help Ava learn how to express her feelings appropriately. If she works hard in therapy, the feelings may become real.
- Therapy can help Ava build her self- esteem once she understands why she constantly needs attention, why she dresses provocatively in order to attract it.
- Ava would benefit from group therapy, so she sees how she affects others.

Tools: Is Your Partner a Charismatic Cheater?

1. Do your partner's emotions seem shallow? Lack conviction?
2. Does your partner flirt to the point of acting seductive around your friends or relatives?
3. Does your partner flaunt his/her physical appearance to get attention and affection from others?

4. Does your partner's style of speech change depending on whom she/he is with?
5. Have you noticed that your partner's emotions shift rapidly for no apparent reason? Crying one moment and laughing the next.
6. Does your partner's personality shift to shape the people she/he is around?
7. Do you have a hard time trusting your partner around your friends and relatives?

If you answered yes to four or more of the questions above, you may be with a charismatic cheater.

8

ESCAPIST CHEATER
MALE

Rob

"I spent most of the day at the hospital with your mother," Val told Rob. "She's doing a bit better, the doctors are saying she may have at least a year left."

They were sitting at the dining room table with the children and Rob was unplugged from his family. Ten-year old Jimmy and eight-year old Jane were talking about their day at school.

"Did you say something?"

"What's the point?" Val said. "You never listen—you're always off in your own world." She got up from the table and stomped out of the room.

"I think Mom is mad at you," Jimmy said.

Rob didn't register—he was fully engrossed in his thoughts. He was going to see Missy in a few hours. He'd told Val he was going out of town for a business trip that evening, which was true. He hadn't told her that his business associate, Missy, was going on the same business trip.

Rob and Missy were a dynamic duo at the office, and

Missy was nothing like Val—she had a great personality, she never got angry, she never yelled or nagged him.

The kids' background noise got louder.

"Give me that back!" Jimmy yelled.

"Ouch, Dad, Jimmy hit me!" Jane cried. Rob turned in time to see his daughter punch Jimmy in his stomach.

"Both of you get to your rooms," Rob yelled. "I can't deal with you two."

Jane ran up the stairs. The dog barked. Jimmy was still on the floor. Rob looked around the house—it was an absolute mess.

What did Val do all day? Missy's house would never look like this.

He was always so relaxed with Missy—she had such a carefree way about her. He never felt any pressure from her. He couldn't remember the last time he'd felt like that at home.

Rob and Missy would talk for hours on end, and they couldn't keep their hands off each other. He couldn't remember the last time he had more than a one-sentence conversation with Val. He certainly couldn't recall the last time he and Val had sex.

Rob and Missy were flying into Chicago. Rob had done his research: not only had he found the best restaurant, he'd also booked a five-star hotel right by the lake so they could take a stroll after dinner, holding hands. He couldn't get that romantic walk out of his head. He smiled, went upstairs and shaved again to make sure he had the clean look he liked. He changed clothes. He'd thought of every detail. He had a bouquet of Missy's favorite flowers and a bottle of her favorite chardonnay sent to the room. He'd even had them put the chardonnay on ice so it would be properly chilled by the time they arrived.

Rob planned a shopping excursion for Missy the next day—she loved to shop, he loved the smile on her face when she was happy. It sure beat Val's sour look. When he finished shaving he saw Val packing his suitcase. She'd packed his suitcase for fourteen years now. If Val didn't pack it Rob would always forget something.

"Don't forget your laptop," she said.

Rob looked at her. Why was she always wearing those sweat pants? Would it kill her to throw on a little bit of makeup once in a while? Missy would never let herself go like that.

When Val turned around to grab his plane ticket for him, Rob noticed she'd put on more weight. She really had a big ass. She'd been heavier ever since the children were born. Val used to be small and svelte like Missy, but those days were long gone.

Rob thought about how proud he'd feel with Missy on his arm when all the heads in the restaurant turned to look at her.

"So do you have it?" Val asked.

"Have what?"

"Your notes for your presentation?"

"What are you, my mother?" Rob said as he walked down the stairs, suitcase in hand. He let the front door slam behind him.

He was finally out of the house, away from Val and the chaos. Within a few hours, Missy was turning heads in the restaurant with her tight black dress. Just as they were toasting over their appetizer, a man walked up to their table with a large envelope.

Back at home, Val had tucked the kids into bed, said prayers with them, given each a goodnight kiss, and let the dog out. As soon as the dog was in, she locked up and sank down on the couch.

She felt tears stream down her cheek. She'd have to call a locksmith tomorrow to change the locks. Rob would no longer be welcome after the divorce papers were served to him in the Chicago restaurant.

Rob's Meeting:

It was Rob's second session in my office and he continued to talk incessantly about his ex-girlfriend Missy. "I have to get her back," he kept saying.

Rob looked disheveled, his clothes wrinkled, his hair uncombed. He smelled like he hadn't showered for days.

"I don't care that the dumb, fat bitch is leaving me," he said. "She can have everything. The kids, the money, the house, even the damn dog. I don't care about any of it. Only Missy." He shifted in his chair. "One more time," he said. "That was the end."

"One more time for what?" I asked.

"Missy," he said. "She asked if I would fuck her one more time. I can never say no to Missy. She was lying in the bed naked and she looked so perfect. I had to have her one more time."

"What happened?" I asked. I could see he was cringing as he told the story.

"I had a meeting with our biggest account at nine sharp. The alarm clock never rang—even though I *know* I set it—and when I woke up Missy was gone and it was nine-fifteen. I jumped out of bed, threw on my suit, and ran out onto the street in a panic to catch a cab. When I finally found one I was still fifteen minutes away—stuck in traffic.

"I called the company to explain I was going to be late. Mr. Black's assistant told me there were thirty people in the meeting room waiting for my presentation.

"I've never felt so helpless in my life. We finally arrived at 9:42. I swear the elevator stopped on every floor. So I run into the office waiting room and Mr. Black's assistant says he dismissed the meeting, didn't want to see my presentation—or me, ever again.

"Then she tells me Missy was scheduled to handle the presentation instead. I was flabbergasted—and would you believe Missy walked right past me without saying a word? When I got back to the hotel room, all her stuff was gone. Guess who was promoted to my position after I lost my job?"

"Missy?"

"Can you believe it?" he asked.

"Sounds like the love of your life set you up and literally screwed you so she could get your job."

"I found out she was also sleeping with my boss, and he wanted to get rid of me. In spite of it all, I can't live without her. I need to win her back."

Rob's Background:

Rob's father was a perfectionist surgeon who was absent from the home most of the time. When he appeared, he found fault with whatever Rob was doing and preached to him about excellence. His mother was an overly critical woman who was hard on the hired help and her children. Their rooms were never clean enough; they never did their schoolwork fast enough, got grades high enough, and so on.

Behind closed doors it was a tense, critical household with parents who had no love for each other. To the outside world it was a beautiful home with successful parents and extraordinarily gifted children.

Rob learned the value early on of fooling the public, of the false façade and the importance of keeping up appearances. He wanted to be known as running a tight ship in his neighborhood, wanted the neighbors to know everything at home was in order and life was good. That wasn't true. Life was not good. He was disinterested in his wife and in love with another woman.

Rob's Assessment:

Rob was obviously using Missy, the object of his affection, to escape reality. Nothing else matters to Rob at this time. He isn't taking any of the important things into consideration, including his wife, children, or career. His obsession with Missy has ruined his life, yet he's still trying to lure her back into that life.

A psychiatrist eventually assessed Rob and diagnosed him with obsessive-compulsive disorder. Medication, along with cognitive behavioral therapy from me, has lessened Rob's obsessive thoughts. Nevertheless, he has a hard time concentrating and has since been diagnosed with depression.

As his obsessive-compulsive thoughts decreased, he realized he'd lost his wife, kids, and job all in a matter of weeks. In addition, the object of his affection was the woman who screwed him over to get his job.

Rob's Recommendations:

- Rob should continue individual therapy.
- He would benefit from family therapy with his children.
- Rob should continue to learn how to deal with his obsessions through thought stopping cognitive behavioral therapy. For example, he can learn how to picture a stop sign in his head every time he thinks of his object of infatuation. Soon the stop signs become automatic in Rob's cognitive thought process.
- Rob needs to address his depression through therapy and medication (if indicated).
- Rob and his ex-wife would benefit from counseling, as they still have to raise two children together.

- Rob could benefit from group therapy, which could help him learn how to maintain a healthy relationship.

Tools: Are You an Escapist Cheater?

1. Do you use your object of affection to escape reality? Does he or she keep your mind from focusing on your problems?
2. Are you unable to focus for long periods of time and find it hard to complete tasks? Do people say you have become distant?
3. Are you excessively devoted to your object of affection, to the point that it interferes with everyday functioning?
4. Do you show rigidity and stubbornness when you feel the relationship with your object of affection is compromised?
5. Do you put your object of affection on a pedestal, seeing her/him as perfect and without flaws? For example, Rob saw Missy as perfect and projected his own imperfections himself onto Val.
6. Do you spend hours of your time thinking about and planning events for your object of affection?
7. Have you found yourself ignoring important people in your life because of your object of

affection? For example, Rob was ignoring his wife, kids, dog, and his sick mother.

8. Are you convinced you would be miserable without your object of affection?
9. If your object of affection does not return a phone call or an e-mail/text right away, do you start to panic?

If you answered yes to five or more of these questions, you may be an Escapist Cheater.

9

ESCAPIST CHEATER
FEMALE

Pam

Why did I ever get married? Pam shifted in her seat. *I must have been crazy.*

Pam and Mark were on their way to a company holiday party, and Pam was certain everyone but her would be in the holiday spirit. She looked over at Mark's hands as he grabbed the steering wheel. Hard to believe this was the guy who charmed her in college when he played basketball and wore a letterman jacket. Now she couldn't stand him—she couldn't stand those long, bony fingers.

"Honey, you look beautiful tonight," he said. "You make me so proud to take you anywhere." He smiled at her, then went back to watching the road.

It was getting slippery with the light dusting of snow.

God—they look like Ichabod Crane's hands. How can I get the man new hands? I can't. I'm stuck with this, married to a man with Ichabod Crane hands. He'll touch me and try to caress me with those hands. What can I do? I want a divorce. I'm sorry, Judge, I just couldn't let the hands of Ichabod Crane touch me, I'm sure the court will understand.

"Jim Peterson will be there tonight," Mark said. "I told you Barnes & Co. hired him, didn't I?"

"Which Jim Peterson, dear?" She overemphasized the dear. If she slipped some kind of Nutri-Hunk protein powder in his morning coffee, would that flesh out his bony fingers?

"Remember? He played guard with me at Purdue," he said. "You always thought he was too good for Candy Alverez."

"Oh, her, yeah, she was a bitch. She kind of had front teeth like a beaver, didn't she?"

"Well, I always thought she was nice, and she took female state championship in tennis that year, went pro after that. They're still married."

"I didn't remember that he married her."

"Yeah, but I think they're having some tough times. Looks like he's getting a divorce, which is too bad. They have two little children."

"A shame," she said.

She was playing with him—her Ichabod Crane husband with the bony fingers. Of course she remembered Jim Peterson. She wanted Jim the moment she saw him. But he didn't respond to her flirting at the pre-game party when they were in college. He asked Candy to dance instead. That's when Mark came over, and Pam danced with him to get noticed by Jim. She remembered Jim, oh yes. Now there was a stud. She'd fantasized about him many times.

They arrived at the party of more than a thousand

people, held at their local country club. As soon as they handed over their coats the president of the company put his arm around Mark.

"Mark, I want you to meet someone. Dick Cheney is in the lobby." Mark left Pam standing by the coat rack as he waltzed away with his boss.

Jim saw her right away.

"Pam, you look awesome," he said.

"Thanks, Jim, so do you."

"You were right about Candy. You warned me."

"Oh? I don't remember," she said.

"Liar." He smiled.

"Okay, I thought you were too good for her. Happy? Is your fishing expedition over now?"

"Not yet." He looked into her eyes. "You know, I thought Mark won the Grand Prize when he got you."

"Is Candy here?"

"Somewhere," Jim said. "She's along for appearances. For some reason people think it's a big deal to be married to a pro tennis star."

Pam giggled. "Does she still have beaver teeth?"

"Nope. She spent over seventy thousand on caps. They look great on TV, but in person her teeth will blind you if you look directly at them." She laughed. "Come with me?" Jim said.

"I can't leave."

"We'll only be gone a second."

"Okay."

When the valet brought his new Hummer to the curb Jim tipped him and helped Pam into the car.

"What are we doing here, Jim?"

"Just sit tight. We'll be right back."

"I've never been in a Hummer," she said as she fastened her seat belt. "This is cool."

He pulled over on the long country club drive.

"What are you doing?" she asked.

"You drive." He got out of his seat and went around to the passenger door. Now that he was on the ground and she was seated, he looked at her face to face, almost close enough to kiss her.

"Me?" she asked.

"Sure, you'll love it. Try it."

"Great. Okay." She got into the driver's seat and buckled up. "Geeze, we sit so high here—this is cool, Jim. It's like being in heaven and driving from a cloud."

Jim gave her directions and she followed them, going down a country road.

"It's quiet," he said.

"Yeah." She focused on the road, feeling like she could plow through a military attack in her vehicle.

"Now drive naked," he said.

"What?"

"You heard me. Drive naked. I dare you."

"Oh, Jim."

"Remember when we played Dare at the frat house?"

"I went home early that night. It was getting too wild for me."

"Make it up to me, then. Drive naked," he said.

She pulled over to a little cove off the side of the road and stopped the car.

"What are you doing? You really want to see me naked?"

"You're beautiful, Pam. I've always wanted you."

"Do you still want me?"

"Yes." She noticed how the moonlight made a few gray hairs in his sideburns shimmer. He had a beautiful smile and a strong, confident manner.

She looked down at his hands—perfectly normal man's hands. She imagined life with Jim instead of Mark. He'd be divorced and all the wealth of the tennis world would provide a luxurious lifestyle for her, even better than the life she and Mark worked so hard to afford.

Jim kissed her and in moments he was peeling off her dress. With the engine running and the lights off, he slid his pants to his ankles. Pam straddled his lap, not completely removing her low-cut black dress. The sex was hot, and she felt like the foreplay had started ten years ago.

Jim and Pam screamed together at the top of their lungs. Luckily they couldn't be heard in the woods.

"I'll have my own place in January," he said. They pledged to meet again.

They dressed to return to the party and decided to go in one at a time. While the car waited in line for the valet, Pam looked at Jim's feet. *God, they're big.* Had to be a size 15 or 16. She started thinking about how scary feet like that would be without shoes.

"I'll call soon," he said.

Don't. Don't call. Or call again when your feet shrink. Those feet

would take up all the sheets. *I won't be in a bed with a guy with feet like that. Forget it.*

"Sure, Jim. Here's my cell phone." She gave him her phone number with one digit off.

"Thanks for the great feet," she said.

"Great feet?"

"I meant great time, sorry. I had a great time."

She turned and walked away. *That only worked tonight because I didn't see his feet. If I'd seen them, it wouldn't have happened at all. Yuck!*

Mark never really missed her at the party. There were so many rooms, so many things to do, and Pam gazed at many young male guests thinking any one of them could be the one.

Pam's Meeting:

Pam walked into my office dressed to perfection. She was very thin, petite, with short red hair and a pinched face.

"I'm thirty-five, Dr. Wood. I've had issues since my mid-twenties."

"What issues?" I asked.

"Bulemia. Off and on since I was about seventeen. I was diagnosed with Body Dysmorphic Disorder."

"What brings you in today?" I asked.

"I want to divorce my husband," she said.

"How long have you been married?" I asked.

"About fourteen years."

"Why do you want to divorce him?"

"Well, there are several reasons, but no therapy is going to fix the fact that he has bony hands."

"Does that seem a logical for divorce to you?"

"I'm literally disgusted by his hands. They remind me of Ichabod Crane, Dr. Wood, and I can't bear to let his bony hands touch my body. And you wouldn't either!"

"When his hands touch your body, explain to me how it makes you feel," I said.

"I feel nauseous. Literally nauseous," she said. "Like fingers on a chalk board, it makes all the hair on the back of my neck stand straight up."

"What is your sex life like with Mark?" I asked.

"Sex?" she said. "We don't do that, we haven't had sex for years. I can't let him touch me with those disgusting digits."

Pam's Background:

Pam was born a twin in a family of eight children. There was never enough of anything and she was given hand-me-down everything's. Scholastically, she was a high achiever and received a scholarship to college, but there was never enough money to buy new clothes and she often stayed away from events as a result. If trying to win the attention of someone she liked, she often missed the opportunity with her second-hand clothes.

People tended to keep Pam at arm's length, and vice versa—she had a hard time getting close to others. When she met Mark, she thought him a good candidate for a husband but found it hard to get close to him. Her insecurities about her body have followed her into her adult life. She's preoccupied with her clothing and meticulous in her dress.

Pam's Assessment:

Pam doesn't want to face the reality that she has a poor relationship with her husband. If she admits it's flawed, then she'll be at fault. Instead, Pam creates a problem with her husband's bony hands and obsesses about them. This defense mechanism functions as a diversion from her own issues while shielding Pam from blame for any problems in the marriage.

Perhaps it's the lack of communication, little to no sexual contact, or feelings of inadequacy that led Pam on the road to obsession. She endures recurrent, intrusive thoughts about Mark's bony hands and is so fearful of being overweight that she binges and purges.

It should be noted that Pam doesn't recognize her disgust over Mark's hands as an irrational thought. Mark may have many redeeming qualities, none of which can be appreciated while Pam is so focused on his fingers.

When she meets her old flame Jim at the country club party, she has a spontaneous affair. The excitement represents her search to escape her marriage and find a better relationship. By focusing on the size of his feet, she is unconsciously avoiding intimacy.

Pam is often preoccupied with perfection and finds herself intolerant of anyone who isn't perfect. She has no idea that she's projecting her insecurity onto others. She experiences relationship difficulties due to rigid thought patterns she seems unable to control. What's more, her relationship difficulties and issues with imperfection seem to become worse with age and stress, due to an inability to be flexible and compromise.

Since Pam is stressed about her marriage and has been contemplating divorce, her obsession over her husband's hands—a metaphor for the imperfection of their marriage—has intensified.

Pam's Recommendations:

- Pam should seek cognitive behavioral therapy to get over her obsessions.
- She would benefit from individual therapy to uncover the root of her irrational issues and address as well her depression and anxiety. Most important, therapy can help Pam learn what she's trying to escape and address the issue.
- She and her husband would benefit from couples counseling.
- Pam and her husband would benefit from sex therapy.
- Pam needs to learn how to neutralize irrational and obsessive thoughts with other thoughts or actions.
- Pam may want to look into taking psychiatric medication to control her obsessive thought process.

Tools: Are You an Escapist Cheater?

1. Do you have negative thoughts about your partner's appearance or habits that cause you constant distress?
2. Do you worry constantly about your partner's behavior or habits even though you know they aren't significant?
3. Do you have a difficult time getting rid of obsessive thoughts about your partner?
4. When you obsess about your partner does it relieve the other stressors that are going on in your life?
5. Do you obsess about your partner numerous times per day?
6. Have others told you that you obsess too much about your partner's issues?
7. Has your partner gotten upset with your obsessions?
8. Do you find yourself thinking you'd be better off with a partner who doesn't come with your current partner's imperfections?

If you answered yes to more than four questions you may be an Escapist Cheater.

10

DOWN-LOW FEMALE
CHEATER

Jada

"Jada, stay with me," Morgan said.

"I can't," she said. "I have to go by school and pick-up my check this morning."

"You have all day," he said. "Come on, honey, can't I do anything to coax you to stay?"

She was up, put on a turtleneck and was sliding up her jeans. "I'm afraid not."

"Wait, look, I'm wearing my sexy-come-back-to-bed look," he smiled.

"I see that, it's really something, Morgan, but I have to go," she smiled at him.

"It was an excellent try, but you know how I am. I'm very task-oriented."

"Well, let's see if I can't get on your agenda more often. I'm a hot commodity, you know," he said.

"Oh, you see one college quarterback, you've seen them all," she fliply said.

He stood up laughing, picked her up, and put her on

the bed and playfully pinned her down. "Well, tonight, let me show you how unique I am, Jada," he said.

"Okay, okay," she laughed. "Tonight then. But you have to let me go."

He let her go, and then grabbed the engagement ring. "Don't forget your ring."

"Oh, yeah," she put the beautiful one carat rock on her finger.

"You're mine, Jada," he held her tenderly. "You have my heart."

"Likewise," she said as he kissed her goodbye.

Morgan stood by the door watching Jada walk away from his apartment then went to his window as she walked toward campus. He hadn't planned to get married so soon after college— it's just that love blindsided him.

Jada was gorgeous, smart, kind, and their chemistry just clicked. He was crazy about her. He wished she was a little more passionate in their lovemaking, but it was all pretty new to her, Jada had very little experience in bed.

Morgan decided he would rather his girlfriend have too little experience, than too much. He knew he could have that with her, if he was patient.

Jada went in to the administration office to pick up her check. When she twirled around to walk out, she bumped right into a girl going into the admin office.

"Sorry," Jada said. "My fault. I have to watch where I'm going."

"No, it's okay," she said in awe at the beautiful girl

she ran into. She had the most beautiful soft-looking skin and huge brown eyes, and rosy pink cheeks.

Jada did not back away quickly; she had seen her before somewhere on campus. But now she found herself starring at this girl's dreamy green eyes. As she did she felt a flutter and felt confused. *Why was she reacting this way, to some pretty white girl?*

"Oh, you're in my marketing class with Phillips, I think," Jada said.

"Uh-huh. Michelle Wentz," she said.

"Nice to meet you, I'm Jada Jones," Jada said.

In moments they were walking to marketing class together, getting to know each other and laughing about the way the Professor Phillips lisped and banged his stick on the board.

They caught lunch together a couple of times in the Union, and the girls found themselves becoming fast friends. Jada didn't talk much about Morgan or her engagement, but she did mention him. Michelle was just not too interested in her romantic life, so they talked about other interests and always they found things to laugh about.

Shortly after that Michelle asked Jada if she would come help her with her wardrobe. "I have some stuff that I've had since middle school, I swear. Can you help me go through what I need to toss?"

"Sure," Jada agreed. "Morgan's got an away game this weekend. Should I come over Friday?"

"Great, I'll fix some dinner for us," she said.

Jada arrived on Friday with wine. The two great

friends poured a glass and toasted to a wardrobe for the new millennium.

"Okay Jada, you sit in the chair," Michelle said. "It's cushy and you can give me a thumbs up or thumbs down when you see it on me."

She walked into her closet and came out in very tight jeans and an oversized sweater.

"Great for cleaning a garage in the fall, but we have no garage, lose the sweater, lose the jeans," Jada said.

Michelle kicked a laundry basket out and from the closet tossed the sweater and jeans. She came out in a short jean skirt and shirt she tied in front.

"Down south cute. Absolutely not. Toss them," she said.

This time Michelle dropped them in the basket and turned so Jada could see how perfect her figure was from behind.

"Wow, Michelle, you have it going on from the back here," Jada said as she tipped her wine.

Michelle came out wearing a shear blouse that was all open in front. "How about the front. Do you think I have it going on in the front too?"

Jada was stunned. She had been hoping for a moment like this but didn't want to admit it to herself. Michelle opened her blouse to show Jada her breasts; she took a few steps towards Jada.

There was silence and tension and desire building between them. Then finally Jada reached to touch them. She rubbed them and then she started to kiss them.

In moments the girls were entwined on Michelle's

bed, kissing each other passionately. Then Jada pulled back. "Morgan can't ever know, Michelle. I'm going to marry him," she said.

"Of course, and don't tell my boyfriend either," Michelle said.

"I won't. The girls continued their session throughout the weekend, and a number of weekends to come.

They decided it was best to lay low on campus and avoid each other, so that no rumors would ever get started. But they continued to find times when they could meet under the guise of studying together at each other's apartments, when they were really spending their time naked and loving one another.

Each time retreating to heterosexual lovers, but truly feeling more for each other, than they did their men—who never suspected a thing.

Jada's Meeting

Jada made an appointment with me over the phone. She told me that she was having issues with her sexual orientation.

As she arrived at her first appointment, she appeared a bit apprehensive. She walked around the office and commented on the number of books that I had. She asked me if I had read all of them and I assured her that I had.

She stated that she was engaged and extended her hand so that I could see her ring.

"I'm living a lie," she said. "I'm having an affair with

a woman. I love my fiancé, Morgan, but I won't stop my affair with Michelle. Is that okay to do and still get married?" she asked.

"I've been attracted to women as long as she could remember," Jada said. "My sex life with Michelle is loving, gentle, and magical."

"I adore Morgan, he loves me very deeply," she said. "But I feel more and more distant from him as time goes on."

"I can't see me marrying a man, I would be forced to live a lie every day of my life," she said. "But keeping a secret life, is difficult also. We have to keep our relationship hidden. How long can I do that? I want to cry, Dr. Wood, but I have no more tears."

Jada's Background:

Jada remembers liking girls on her soccer and basketball team. She said there were numerous times that she felt odd or unusual while all the girls in school were dating boys and talking incessantly about their boyfriends or boy crushes. Jada felt no desire to date guys.

Jada remembers a boy in junior high asking her to a dance and she said, 'no'. She said the boy was hurt by her rejection. She said after that there were rumors that Jada was a lesbian.

She said that people who she thought were her friends started avoiding her. She recalls crying herself to sleep for weeks. Jada stated that the next dance she was asked to attend, she went.

She recalled that her friends no longer avoided her,

and she quit hearing the gossip, as she would walk down the school halls. Jada said that she has had a boyfriend ever since, and she never wants to face that type of discrimination again.

She also said that she thought her family would disown her, if they knew that she was bisexual. "How do you think it feels, Dr. Wood, to be a black lesbian?" Jada asked.

Jada's Assessment:

Jada is bisexual, but she does not want to let others know that she is bisexual. She is afraid that the heterosexual community will shun her. Jada already has experienced discrimination due to her skin color. Jada has said that she in not ready to share her secret affair with anyone, including her fiancé Morgan. Jada has openly admitted that she prefers to be with females, however, she likes to have sex with Morgan as well.

Jada said what bothers her most is the guilt that she feels toward Morgan. She feels torn apart inside for living a double life.

She has a deep-seated fear of getting caught or her relationship with Michelle being discovered. Jada is also fearful that her family will reject her if they were aware that she was bisexual.

Jada's Recommendations:

- Jada needs to attend individual therapy sessions and talk about her feelings of guilt.

- Jada needs to decide if marrying Morgan is the right thing to do at this point.
- She would benefit from becoming more educated on the gay or bisexual community.
- She needs to get in touch with her authentic self.
- Jada would benefit from extended family therapy as she feels that her family has a very conditional love for her.
- Morgan and Jada would benefit from couple's therapy.
- Michelle and Jada would also benefit from couple's therapy.
- Jada may want to address some of her issues about her African-American heritage.

Tools: Are you a Down-Low Cheater?

1. Have you been sexually attracted to members of the same sex for a number of years?
2. Do you find that you are living a double life, and engaging in sexual affairs with members of the same sex?
3. Do you find that you would rather be with someone of the same sex?
4. Do you lie about not being attracted to individuals of the same sex?
5. Are you like Jada and just want a relationship that looks good in society's eyes, so you hide your gay identity?

6. Do you find that you are secretly going to gay bars and other gay venues to acquire a sexual encounter?

7. Most of the time do you regret that you cannot be openly gay to your loved ones?

8. Do you feel like you are living a lie in your home and family life because you are acting as if you are not attracted to members of the same sex?

If you answered yes to four or more of these questions you maybe the Down-Low Cheater.

11

DOWN-LOW CHEATER
MALE

Spencer

"Longfellow University Rule Number 10. This should go without saying. You'll be given a playbook. It is against our code, our team rules and regulations, and God's universal law to share your playbook, or any proprietary information from our team. Is that clear?"

"Yes, Coach." The thirty-five university football team members all nodded.

It was day one of the new team's training and he came on hard to get the team's attention. It was an honor to be coached by balls-to-the-wall Spencer Turner. The man was a football legend, with the appeal of a man's man and looks that made women swoon.

"We've got a long way to go this year. I can tell from practice we've got some pansies in here. Anyone who didn't get all their gear, let my assistants hear about it. Now run two miles around the track and shower up. Get out of here."

Spencer stood next to Preston and Ramon, his two

graduate assistant coaches. "What do you think? Will we make the play-offs this year?"

They discussed the team's prospects until Spencer's cell phone rang.

"What, honey?" he asked.

"Spence, I thought you were leaving on Saturday morning," his wife of fifteen years said. "That flight gets you in before the conference starts. You don't have your things, do you?"

"Took my bags this morning, Donna. I'm flying out after school."

"Doesn't the conference start on Saturday?" she asked.

"Yes, it's a day earlier or so, but I got a cheaper flight and I have to watch my budget. It's even with the extra hotel nights."

"What are you going to do there?" she asked.

"Meet with a few recruiters before the conference," he said. "Besides, honey, you can use a break from me. It's the season. You know I'm only thinking football anyway."

"I know," she said.

"I'll see you on Tuesday then, babe."

"I love you, Spencer."

"Right back at you, Donna. You're the only girl for me. Tell Sissy and George I'll miss them."

"I will. 'Bye, honey."

"I'll call every night."

Spencer's two-hour flight was uneventful. He checked into a charming San Francisco hotel, showered and shaved, then struck a pose in front of the mirror.

"You look pretty damn good for your age." He stroked himself. "Solid arms, great pecs, you look a lot younger than you are. *Damn, Donna's a lucky woman.* "

He wrapped a towel around himself and began to dance in front of the mirror—happy to have the freedom to act silly, let his crew-cut hair down. There was a knock on his door. He looked out the peephole and smiled.

It was his friend Jerry, the coach from Texas Tech.

"Come on in, Jerry. Beer?"

"Sure, thanks. Heard you were in early for the conference." Jerry eyed Spencer in his towel. "You working out with the team? You look pretty buff."

"Think so?" Spencer removed his towel and turned around.

"Sure do," Jerry said.

Spencer made no move to put the towel back. Instead he walked past Jerry and stood near the room's self-service honesty bar. With his back turned he stroked his cock.

Jerry sat down nearby in a chair. He was a strong young coach with a well-built body. He'd been a quarterback in the pros and always had good press.

With his back still turned Spencer stroked his cock some more and bent over the cooler to look inside.

"See anything else you want, Jerry? I got Beer Nuts in here."

By the time Jerry came over to the cooler he had pulled his shirt off and unzipped his pants. He put his hands on Spencer's bare ass and started to rub his backside and fondle Spencer's balls from behind.

"I want to fuck you," Jerry whispered in his ear.

"You talk too much," Spencer said.

In moments the men were locked in a sexual grip that erupted several times that night.

In a quiet moment later in the evening, Spencer said, "Jerry, I've really missed you. I can't stop thinking about you."

"Me, too," Jerry said. "What are we going to do?"

"Everything's perfect the way it is, Jerry. I don't want to change a thing. My kids need their mom. What about you? Does your wife suspect?"

"Not a clue," Jerry said. "What do you do when I'm not around?"

"Health Club, or a porn shop," Spencer said. "You?"

"The same," Jerry said.

Spencer found time to visit a health club and a popular porn shop in the Castro area before he left San Francisco.

On the way back he reflected on what he'd told Jerry. It was true: everything in his life *was* perfect. He had the freedom to travel whenever he wanted and never needed to look hard for a fresh young partner. At home he was a loving husband to Donna and a great father to their kids. Okay, so sometimes he felt like a fraud, but it went with the territory.

"Hi, I'm McKenna," said the friendly young blonde seated next to him on the plane.

"Spencer," he said.

"I've never been to Denver," she lied.

She was actually a private investigator from Denver.

Her briefcase already held photos taken on Castro Street, at a health club, and at a restaurant where Spencer and Jerry had enjoyed a candlelight dinner.

Donna's Meeting:

Donna came into my office holding her stomach. "I'm going to be sick," she said. Her eyes were swollen and her face was stained with tears. Spencer walked in beside her, his hand at her back.

"I'm so sorry, baby," he said. "I never meant to hurt you." He turned to me. "Donna had a private detective follow me. She was afraid I was having an affair.""I had no idea he was having an affair with a man!" she said. "Oh, my God, I was in shock."

"I'm sorry," he said.

"I can't believe he's gay or bisexual." Donna shook her head. "How do you explain years of him making love to me?"

"I do love you, Donna," he said.

"If you loved me, you'd never have been sneaking around like you did." She looked up at me. "I got suspicious because he wasn't sexually attracted to me anymore, Dr. Wood. It's been almost a year since the last time we had sex.

"In moments my life has been turned upside down," she said. "I've gone from the prestige of being a coach's wife to backyard gossip. I don't know what's real anymore. My whole marriage has been a façade.

"I thought Spencer and I were in love. We were a

family. Now I find out I've only been window dressing for his charade."

"I'm so sorry, Donna. I never meant to hurt you or the children. I do love you. Stay with me—we can work this out. I'll change. I promise you. I swear, Donna. I'll never do this again."

Donna loves Spencer, but she's a smart woman. She knew Spencer won't—can't—change.

Spencer's Meeting:

Spencer told me he had a sexual relationship with one of his fraternity buddies when he was in college. "I used to play ball with Peyton and we went everywhere together. One night we got drunk and started making out. It ended up with a sexual encounter.

"It might have happened more than that, but Peyton dropped out after the fling, joined the military, and last I heard he'd became a war hero in Iraq."

"I was very attracted to men after that and found myself getting drunk and going to gay bars in nearby big cities. I was a big hit with the older men because of my football status, my age, and my physique.

"I've kept my side sex on the down-low because I was scared of what my family, friends, and society would think of me," he said. "If I'm quiet about my secret, I live the ideal life for me.

"I knew Donna was the one from the minute I met her," he said. "She was a passive, sweet, introverted woman who liked time to herself and trusted me with her whole heart. She was also beautiful and athletic. I tried to be loyal to her, but I found it incredibly difficult as the years went on. When she was pregnant with the first baby, I sought men for sex. Once I started cheating I just couldn't stop. I've been terrified Donna would find out about my other life and divorce me. What'll become of my life? I could lose my career, credibility, family, friends, and children.

"Dr. Wood, what do I do now?"

Spencer's Background:

Spencer knew he was gay when he was twelve years old. He was attracted to the guys on his team and had little interest in getting close to girls. Many times he had to hide his erection when taking showers with other teammates. He often daydreamed about one of his male friends after seeing him naked in the showers.

Spencer said he never felt right acting on his attraction to boys because he didn't know how they would respond. He was self-conscious and secretive—in fact, he kept his secret by dating girls all through junior and senior high school. He was respectful of his dates and gave them goodnight kisses but held off from heavy make-out sessions. "I don't take sex lightly," he told his dates. "I respect you too much. I want to save myself for the right girl."

Most girls played along. Many of them were from religious backgrounds, and none wanted to break the spell of the handsome quarterback interested in them.

"I was popular with the girls," Spencer said, "but I knew I was living a lie."

Spencer told me his father was an authoritarian disciplinarian. "Do it because I'm bigger than you and I told you to do it," was the message he got.

"Dad believed in physical discipline. He hit or spanked my brothers and me on a regular basis."

According to Spencer his mother was a very intelligent, patient, and loving woman. He said he spent most of his free time with his mother when he was a young boy. He said he still gets along well with his mother and they talk on a regular basis.

Spencer's Assessment:

Spencer is gay, not bisexual, because his sexual preference has always been for his own sex. He tries to stay within what he considers societal norms as he's lived two lives, hiding his homosexual encounters. But he's been caught and is at a crossroads: Spencer is now forced to come to terms with his true sexual preference.

Six months after Donna found him out, she and Spencer had separated. They were sharing custody of the children. Spencer was dating men and told me he'd never been happier. He had several male lovers and said he'd like to settle down with one man someday.

He told me he felt like a huge weight had been lifted off his shoulders now that he was no longer living a lie. As for coworkers, friends, and family, Spencer admitted most of them said they weren't surprised and some had suspected he might be gay for a number of years. Oh sure, there were some very unreceptive people as well, but he said they were never true friends if they weren't willing to accept him for who he was.

Spencer's Recommendations:

- Spencer and Donna need to go to couples therapy, regardless of their decision about the marriage, as they have two children to raise.
- Spencer would benefit from individual therapy to work through any guilt about his sexual orientation.
- Spencer, Donna, and the children would benefit from family therapy.
- Since substance use was involved every time Spencer had a homosexual encounter, he may need to be assessed for substance abuse or dependence.
- Donna would benefit from individual therapy, as she needs some time to heal and make rational decisions about her future.
- Donna needs to learn about gay and bisexual relationships, which are foreign to her at this point.
- Spencer and Donna need to keep their relationship friendly for the sake of their children.

Tools: Are You a Down-Low Cheater?

1. Have you been sexually attracted to members of the same sex for a number of years?
2. Do you find that you're living a double life, engaging in sexual affairs with members of the same sex secretly?
3. Do you find that you would rather be with someone of the same sex?
4. Do you lie about being attracted to people of the opposite sex?
5. Do you have a relationship that looks good in society's eyes so you can hide your attraction to your own sex?
6. Have you secretly gone to gay bars and other gay venues to make a sexual connection?
7. At times do you regret that you can't be openly gay to your loved ones?
8. Do you feel like you're living a lie in your home and family life because you're act as if you aren't attracted to members of the same sex?

If you answered yes to four or more of these questions you're a Down-Low Cheater.

12

ADDICTIVE CHEATER (SEXTING) MALE

Brandon

"You mentioned you'd seen orchids used down the arches at the Swanson wedding? I thought you might like to see the photo of it." The florist pulled out a picture of arches covered in gorgeous orchids, with a beaming bride and groom under them.

"I love it, don't you, Brandon?" Tia said.

"Sure, it's really neat, honey. Will I hit my head on that?"

"You shouldn't, it's eight feet on the center and graduates to seven feet on the sides," the florist said. "It's perfect for wedding photos, you'll look very handsome with the wedding party coming down the aisle."

"Works for me. Anything you want, honey." Brandon pulled Tia close and kissed her. His Blackberry went off. He grabbed it, glanced down to see the message, and began texting back.

"Brandon, not again," she said.

"I'm sorry, honey, the market calls."

"You took the afternoon off so we could get our wedding details done today," she said.

"I know, but I want to keep my job, too. It's all part of being a stockbroker. If an important client wants to invest, I got to go. Please forgive me—you know I trust you with all the details. Surprise me." He grinned at Tia and hugged her goodbye.

"I love you," she said.

"Love you too, honey," he said. "Remember I have a tennis game at the club after work, so don't count on me for dinner. I'll call when I'm on my way."

"He's very handsome, you make a beautiful couple," the florist said after Brandon left.

"Thank you, I think so too. If he would just stop working so much, he'd be better than perfect."

"Now for your bouquet, what were you thinking?"

Once outside the florist shop, Brandon pulled up his text message. Sarah T had sent a picture of herself in just her bathing suit bottoms. He enjoyed it for a moment, then texted her again as he got in his car: *Call me.* In moments his phone rang.

"Sarah, who do you think can undress faster, you or me? I'll come over right now."

"Me. I lost the swimsuit bottoms," she said. She sent him a nude shot of herself.

He looked again at the picture. *Oh man, she's so hot.* Hot, great in bed, and they clicked. *She's the best. Well, until she talks. Not so much upstairs, but she's a model. We have lots to talk about when she's horizontal.*

He spent the next couple of hours with her before going over to the Athletic Club for his tennis game. He arrived home in his tennis clothes. Tia hardly missed him.

While gone he'd received texts from four other girls. Two of them he'd already bedded, the other two were on the drawing board. He was still trying to figure out how he would phase out Sarah T and phase in the next shift.

Tia was still The One. That would never change. He loved her. She loved him. He wanted a life and family with her. He craved her. She was the woman he wanted to sleep next to each night. It was just that occasional rolls in the hay with other women were stimulating, and he loved the attention.

"B, I LUV U—"

Another sent a picture of herself taking a shower, one was in lingerie, and one was in a pair of chaps without pants underneath.

It was exciting to text all day to a bevy of women who wanted him. He liked

receiving the half-clothed or naked pictures they sent. What guy wouldn't? Sure, he was in love with Tia, but she didn't know, so it couldn't hurt her. How could it? He was there every night next to her.

These other women were no big deal in the big picture. *Texting, sexting, it's all pretty innocent.* He met women everywhere. They were all over the downtown skyway, in his brokerage firm, downtown bars at happy hour, sports bars, and he'd often go to tennis clubs in different locations where they didn't know Tia. There he could pretend to be a single unattached man and openly flirt.

Then, via texting, he would further the relationship—for the conquest. All of that worked fine until Tia saw a Tyra Banks show that featured a guy texting lots of women while married to another woman.

Tia waited until Brandon went to sleep one night, pulled out his Blackberry, saw the collection of partially clad or nude women, and read the text messages from and to him, trembling.

"BCOB (Brandon, Come Over for Booty)", "SOOK (Sleep Over OK)", "FBJ (Free BJ)", GSH (Get Sex Here)."

Brandon's Meeting:

Brandon sauntered into my office. He was a tall blond man who appeared cocky, but it was obvious to me that his over-confidence was probably due to lack of self-esteem.

Brandon had a ball cap pulled over his eyes and made little eye contact with me. Tia was a petite heavier-set woman with tear stained makeup on her face. Tia brushed her brunette hair back and I could see she was visibly shaken.

Brandon sat on the chair in my office and Tia distanced herself from him and sat on the far end of the couch.

"Brandon has been sexting other women and we are engaged, Dr. Wood. I feel so angry. I hate those sluts they are after my fiancé all the time. You should see the disgusting pictures these women send Brandon. The women have tattoos all over their bodies—one even has a tattoo of Disney world on her back. Women with real class, right, Dr. Wood? How can I marry him when he is excepting all these pictures of half-naked women, I feel abused and disrespected."

"Brandon can you tell me about the text messages?" I asked.

"No big deal, just some chicks with their clothes off. Tia is making a big deal over nothing. I hate it when she gets crazy jealous like this. She needs to chill," he said.

"I am not overreacting. This is disgusting," she said.

"People send sexy messages and pictures on their phones all the time. Tia is insecure about her body. She has to have sex in the dark, and doesn't let me see her naked. I need something to get me off. I'm a dude. Dudes like to look at naked girls. That's a normal thing to do," he said.

"Do you always try to avoid the real issue Brandon?" I asked. "You are using a passive aggressive tactic to make Tia think that what you have done is no big deal, when she says it is a big deal to her. I think it is time to confront this subject. In addition, let's talk about if the two of you really feel that you are ready for marriage."

Brandon crossed his arms, pulled his baseball cap further over his eyes, and stared without expression at the floor. He looked like a defiant teenager who had just been scolded.

Brandon's Background:

Brandon told me his mother found his father cheating on her and left the family when Brandon was seven years old. His father married another woman a year later, and Brandon only saw his mother every other summer and on Christmas.

According to Brandon his stepmother was cold and distant to him. He had no siblings and felt very alone throughout his childhood. He took up tennis to avoid the emptiness of his home life.

Brandon remembers his father cheating frequently on his second wife. Brandon swore he would never tell his stepmother about the affairs he witnessed.

Brandon's Assessment:

Brandon has become addicted to the idea of sex with different women—he's not after just one woman, but several. He doesn't want to hurt his fiancé—he loves Tia but has found it impossible to be monogamous despite his strong feelings for her. The more Tia talks about the wedding and tries to "control" Brandon's life, the more he feels a need to cheat.

Addictive Cheating has very little to do with a person's sexual drive. Cheating becomes addictive when the cheater is constantly, even compulsively, preoccupied with the idea of having sex with people they find attractive.

Most addictive cheaters are seeking action. In Brandon's case, he told me he felt a high that he couldn't get any other way. He said this happened whenever he was talking to, e-mailing, texting or having sex with one of several women that he found attractive. He said he would "throw the line out there" to see if he could get a bite. If he did, he'd continue the pursuit all the way to conquest. According to Brandon, he found women easy to manipulate. Often he'd tell a woman he loved her or say she was his soulmate.

Brandon admitted it became a game for him. The more women he found to seduce, the more women he wanted. The risk grew greater and greater, as did the challenge and excitement of not getting caught.

When he tried to be monogamous with Tia, he'd become restless and bored. He said he often felt depressed, anxious, or guilty after his affairs—but not depressed, anxious, or guilty enough to stop his addictive behavior.

Brandon's Recommendations:

- Brandon needs to be assessed for sexual addiction. Once he understands the condition he needs to talk about it with Tia and be totally honest with her about his behavior.
- Brandon needs individual therapy focusing on his core issues: abandonment and consequent low self-esteem. Brandon must decide if he's willing to work hard in therapy, which for him is an essential step. If therapy proceeds,

ideally Brandon's father should attend several sessions.

- Brandon and Tia need to attend couples therapy.
- Brandon needs to figure out if he can live a lifestyle that is monogamous.

Tools: Are You an Addictive Cheater?

1. Are you preoccupied with having multiple affairs?
2. Do you find it difficult-to-impossible to keep from acting on your sexual impulses?
3. Have you attempted to stop affairs and found that you couldn't?
4. Do you get a rush when thinking about your affairs?
5. Do you find yourself frequently calling, e-mailing, or texting a woman you've had sex with? Many times during the day?
6. Do you spend extensive time and money on your sexual encounters?
7. Do you lie to your partner so you can continue your affairs?
8. Do you have numerous affairs even though you know you could lose your partner, family, or job?
9. Do you find you inevitably lose interest in old sexual relationships and seek out new ones?

10. Have your loved ones expressed concern about your addictive behavior?

If you answered yes to five or more of the above, you may be an Addictive Cheater.

13

ADDICTIVE CHEATER (PORNOGRAPHY) MALE

Bob

Bob had twenty-five years of *Playboy* magazines neatly bound in his collection. His wife, Sandy, didn't mind. Sandy read the jokes or looked at the articles once in a while too, after which Bob carefully put them away again.

Then came the day when Sandy started to clear out the clutter. They had a huge comfortable home in Scottsdale and summered on a lake in Minnesota. All their bills were paid, they had plenty of savings, and Bob would be retiring in another seven years. They'd planned for their retirement and had financial peace of mind.

"Bob, what are we going to do with all these *Playboys*? Can I get rid of them?"

"Leave them alone, they're mine."

"Bob, we're in our fifties. At some point isn't it creepy to be looking at naked girls that could be our grandkids?"

"Just leave them," he said.

"Well, I want to get rid of these shelves and hang art. It'll look so much better." Sandy put her hands on her hips.

"That *is* art," he said.

"Right, eighteen-year-olds naked in the sand. I get it. Why don't you eBay them?"

"Not now." Bob thought he might lose this one if he didn't head out. "I'll be back later."

"We were going to clean the garage today."

"No, I have to go to the office," he said.

"On *Saturday*?"

"Something I should have done this week." He kissed Sandy on the cheek. "See you later."

Bob felt freer as he got in his convertible and felt the spring air in his hair. He thought of his college days when he was the campus stud in a red Corvette. He drove through the ATM and withdrew $500 from his secret account, then headed downtown.

At the Ce Soir Gentleman's Club, a topless hostess named Samantha greeted him warmly and took him by the arm. She had short red hair and he knew she had to be pushing forty, but she was still gorgeous. She had huge assets, long legs, and was so friendly she'd rub her chest against the guests as she seated them.

She walked with him to a front row table. *Rub. Rub. Rub.*

"We missed you yesterday, Bob. Where ya' been?"

"A guy can't skip a day?"

"You don't. We were going to report you missing."

"I took Tish shopping."

"Lucky girl."

"Is Tish working today?" Bob asked.

"She comes on later. Want me to call her for you?" Sam batted her eyes while he ogled her.

"That's okay. I enjoy the variety here."

"We've got a new girl, name's Anna— turned eighteen today. She's on next. The usual?"

"Yes, thank you." He tipped her a twenty.

The waitress brought Bob a screwdriver. He was just settling in when the announcer said, "How about a nice warm welcome for a first time on our stage, Miss Anna Oakley."

She came out dressed as a cowgirl and began a provocative strip around the pole.

Other guys were cheering for her attention, but she crawled on her belly to Bob as he flashed twenty-dollar bills.

She pulled out her G-string at an angle so he could slide in some bills. Anna was exciting—her perfume had a fresh citrus smell that opened his senses. He was so close it seemed like she was dancing just for him.

Anna slowly slid her fringed bra top off and shook her chest. She slid out of her black leather chaps and gyrated her remaining tiny G-string right in front of Bob. She got on all fours in front of him, then lay on her back and spread her legs. Bob left his front row seat to put some bills in her G-string and she held it out for him to take a peek. He could hardly catch his breath it was so arousing to him.

Back home Sandy decided to surprise Bob at work with a pastrami lunch she packed for him. When she asked the security guard where Bob was, he told her Bob didn't work there anymore. He'd been let go over a year ago.

She called Bob's cell phone, but it was turned off. Then she drove downtown—right to the Ce Soir Gentleman's Club, where she saw Bob's car in the parking lot. A nosy neighbor had told her she'd seen his car there more than once and had even seen him going in. Sandy hadn't believed her.

"I'm sorry, no women are allowed," a hostess with a nametag that read "Samantha" told her when she entered. Sandy had to regain her composure if she was going to pull this off. The hostess was topless—and huge.

"I understand, but it might be to your advantage to let this woman in. I'm a reporter for The National Enquirer. We pay $50,000 for a celebrity sighting and $100,000 for a politician. Some insider here's going to make a bundle, might as well be you."

"Wow, I could use that."

"Give me your name and email. I'll email you the details. Then give me a quick tour so I can see the lay of the land here."

"Oh, sure."

Sandy looked around and didn't see Bob anywhere.

"What's behind those beads?" she asked. "Gentlemen can get private lap dances there," Samantha said.

"I've never seen that. Can I peek?"

"Well..."

Sandy slipped Sam a twenty-dollar bill.

"Sure. It's probably important for your article."

The beads rustled and chimed behind her as Sandy

entered and saw Bob seated in a Lazy Boy chair, a young girl wearing only a cowboy hat crawling all over him. Her head was between Bob's knees and her legs spread open—almost in his face. Bob looked as if he were on some euphoric high. He didn't see Sandy. The cowgirl did a U-turn and crawled back up him with her face next to his. He stared at her young perky breasts. Sandy backed out.

"So guys like him, do they come here often?" she asked.

"He's here every day."

"Married?"

"I know he is, because he says his wife is an old bag," Samantha said.

"Really? Poor guy, then."

"No, poor wife. He's mortgaged his house over its value, cleaned out all his savings and 401K—I bet he's gone through more than a million."

"Really?"

"Well, he's kind of keeping one girl. Pays for her townhouse, car payment, and expenses. He takes her shopping and everything."

"What does the wife say?" she asked.

"I think his wife's clueless. Maybe I shouldn't be telling you this—he's one of our biggest customers. Don't put him in your article."

"I won't be writing about that. In fact, I'm not writing about this place. I think it's sad."

"Why are you here, then?" Sam asked.

"I was his old bag," Sandy said.

Sandy's Meeting:

Sandy had just taken a seat in my office when a man started banging on the other side of my ground floor window.

"Let me in!" he screamed. "Sandy, let me in!"

"Don't let that son of a bitch in here." She looked away. "Bob can rot in hell."

"The building is locked, Bob," I told him through the glass. "You aren't coming in."

"You have to let me in. I love Sandy." He started to cry and kept banging on the window.

"Bob, stop it. Go home—if you don't, we'll call the police." The banging stopped, but only so he could talk.

"Sandy, don't you love me? All these years, Sandy, don't you love me? Those girls don't love me. I know that. You were just always too busy for me."

"I was never too busy, but I should have been. He's a lying sack of shit," Sandy said. "I never want to talk with him again." She turned to the window.

"Leave me alone, asshole! Go sell your car, get more lap dances. What a jerk!"

Bang, *bang*, BANG!

"He's burned through all our money, Dr. Wood," Sandy said. "All of it. Our house. Everything we had for retirement. What else am I supposed to do but leave him?

"He's been following me around everywhere. Walmart, 7-Eleven, gas stations, I can't lose him. I thought we would grow old together, now I don't even want to look at him. Call the cops, Dr. Wood. I want him away from me, gone, restrained, in jail—I don't want to ever see him."

"Last call here, Bob, you have to go," I said. I was wasting my breath. He didn't go and he didn't stop banging. I dialed 9-1-1.

"What is the nature of your emergency?"

"I have a distraught husband of my client creating a disturbance in my building and following my client. She wants to file a complaint and get a restraining order. Would you come and remove him?"

Bob knew I'd made the call, but he still kept trying.

"I'll get another job, honey. I still love you. I know you still love me. We can get it back, Sandy."

"Not a chance, not a chance," she said.

In moments lights were flashing, then Bob was taken away in handcuffs. Sandy sat silent for a moment and I saw a tear fall down her cheek.

"Do you still love him?" I asked.

"How can I not?" she whispered. "I've lain next to that man every night for so many years. I don't know what I'd really do without him."

Bob's Meeting:

Private session with Bob after his release from jail:

Bob was sobbing on the couch. I stood up and handed him the box of tissues.

"I can't understand why Sandy would leave me. I did *nothing* to deserve that. I feel so lonely and empty, I feel helpless without Sandy. She used to cook every meal for me. She washed my clothes. We were together for over thirty years. How could she just send me to jail and abandon me? It just doesn't make sense."

"Bob, let's talk about your sex addiction," I said.

"I keep telling you it wasn't an addiction. I just like to look at pretty naked women. Since when is looking at beautiful women an addiction? If that's an addiction, then every straight man in the world would be a sex addict."

"Bob, you've lost almost everything that was dear to you, including your life partner, your home, and the financial security you worked for all your life. How can you deny an addiction?"

"It was Sandy's fault. I swear it is," he said. "She never let me see her naked. I would beg her to leave the lights on, but she said it made her feel uncomfortable. Dr. Wood, do you know that I have *never* seen her body naked and we've been married for over thirty years?

"We've had sex once in the last year—one time. What do you think about that, doctor? Nothing I ever did was good enough for Sandy. I never made enough money and I never felt adequate for her in the bedroom, either. Now the girls at the club—they're different. They can't stay away from me. They *love me* there. All the women there love me. They're attracted to me and they all want to have sex with me, but the manager won't let them."

"They're always telling me how hot I am, crawling all over me. These women are gorgeous, you should see them, and they're nothing like Sandy."

I looked up from taking notes on his comments. "So Bob, our time is almost up, but let me get this straight."

"Sure," he said.

"You think the women at the gentlemen's club are actually in love with you?"He grinned—a delirious grin. "I know they are."

Bob's Background:

Bob grew up in a family that went to church three times a week, didn't allow dancing, and prayed at every turn of their day. When he went away to college his eyes were opened to a whole new world— and he rebelled from his strict upbringing.

A fraternity buddy took him when he was a freshman sixty miles away to a strip club. He saw a nude woman dancing and couldn't believe it was even a possibility to witness this guilty pleasure. The cover charge was high, so Bob couldn't afford to go often, but he would save to go watch the dancers. Along the way he met Sandy, married, and performed well as a father and breadwinner for years.

Sandy gave him the freedom he needed to maintain the Hugh Hefner myth of an older man running around with nude eighteen-year-olds as a "normal" healthy male appetite. But when he was laid off, his ego was shattered and his sex addiction galloped.

He felt old and put out to pasture. The strip clubs made him feel sexual and alive. Even if he wasn't aroused, the people around didn't know that. He could smile or spend time with the girls on shopping trips and feel like a big spender.

In their presence, for a while and whenever he remembered an outing, he wasn't a failure, wasn't getting old, he was fun and sexy and really, really young for his age.

Bob's Assessment:

Bob's mood is up and down. One minute he's talking about how much he misses his wife Sandy, the next minute he's talking about how inadequate she is as a wife. One thing is constant: he's in denial of his sex addiction. Grandiose ideas about his relationship with his objects of affection play into his sexual addiction.

Bob admitted he'd been having problems with premature ejaculation and said this worried him. In addition, he reported he'd had heart problems in the past and was extremely fearful of death.

He also admitted that he needs to be intoxicated before he can be intimate with the young women he meets at the Ce Soir.

Bob's Recommendations:

- In order for Bob to overcome his sexual addiction, he needs to admit that it exists. He would benefit from time spent in sexual rehab, where he could learn from other sex addicts and face the consequences of his addiction.
- Bob needs to assess how his addictive cheating has dominated his life, especially how it has affected his wife.
- Bob needs to admit that the objects of his sexual addiction are not in love with him.

- He needs to get affirmation from venues other than strip clubs.
- Bob and his wife will have to go to couples therapy if they want their marriage to continue. Bob should tell Sandy what he loves about her body.
- Bob should remain in individual therapy to address the core issues underlying his addiction, such as abandonment.

Bob and Sandy's Recommendations in Marriage Therapy:

- Sandy needs therapy to work on self-esteem issues.
- Sandy and Bob would both benefit from sensate focus, a set of exercises designed to have partners focus on their own sensual enjoyment in interacting and pleasuring each other rather than intercourse and orgasm.
- Sandy would benefit from attending some therapy sessions with Bob to
- discuss her insecurities and learn about Bob's.
- Sandy needs to go out of her comfort zone and learn to feel sexual again.
- She can stand in front of a mirror and really appreciate her body. She should know that her partner might be as insecure about body issues as she is.

Tools: Are You a Sex Addict?

1. Do you objectify women or men on a regular basis?
2. Are you obsessively fearful about losing your sexuality?
3. Do you have an extreme fear of death?
4. Do you find that the older you get, the younger the age gap when you have sex outside your committed relationship?
5. Does your partner feel that you don't respect him or her?
6. Have you lost large amounts of money to your sexual addiction?
7. Have you lost time due to your sexual addiction?
8. Does your partner worry about your sexual addiction?

   If you answered yes to four or more of these questions you may be an addictive cheater.

14

PUPPETEER CHEATER
MALE

Carl

Karen knew she was driving too slowly but she dreaded going home to Carl. He'd question her until she felt even more tired and defeated than she was now. Her cell phone rang three times. The third time she answered.

"What is it, Carl?"

"Where are you?"

"I'll be home in a few minutes," she said.

"Hurry up. I'm waiting for you."

Karen hung up the phone and drove home with tears streaming down her cheeks. She felt like a prisoner in her own house. Ever since Carl lost his job, her life had become unbearable.

Carl had been married before, to a woman named Marguerite who never opened her mouth. There was no challenge, little interaction, and he thought about getting rid of her only days after their wedding. Instead he opted for extra-marital affairs. Marguerite, who knew that Carl screwed around with some of his female patients, surprised Carl by hiring a well-known divorce attorney who got her a handsome settlement. She moved to Mexico and never looked back.

Carl was ten years Karen's senior and had been her therapist four years ago. At the time Karen and her husband, Troy, were seeing Carl for couples counseling. Carl suggested Karen and Troy separate for a few months. He continued therapy sessions with Karen, who was devastated at the thought of losing Troy. Karen felt like a failure—an undesirable failure, a wife with no sex appeal. She would tell Carl about her insecurities and her fear of being alone. In fact, she told Carl everything. He was her therapist. She trusted him.

Carl's intimate knowledge about Karen made her vulnerable to his control and manipulation. When the affair began, Karen wasn't aware that psychologists have to wait at least two years after terminating therapy with a client to have a relationship. She was aware that Carl had taken a liking to her. In their third private therapy session, he started wearing designer suits and combing his hair to the side to make it less obvious that he was balding.

Karen was flattered by Carl's attention and compassion. After one session she spent crying over Troy, Carl said, "Do you need a hug?"

"A hug would be nice," she said. So the hug became a regular part of Karen's therapy.

One day while he hugged her, she felt Carl's hand slip to her long toned thigh. At the time she was so distraught that the attention felt nice. By the sixth week of therapy, Karen was showing up in lower-cut tops and shorter skirts. She often caught Carl glancing down her blouse or checking out her legs. As she became more comfortable with therapy, Carl became more comfortable with Karen. He rubbed her shoulders, which escalated into backrubs.

Karen found herself not wearing a bra to some of her sessions. Carl would glance at her breasts as she talked, but only briefly. He still maintained a professional relationship as they talked about her separation, which soon led to a messy divorce.

"Karen, do you mind if I sit on the couch while we talk?" Carl asked one day. "I think it could be therapeutic if you had unconditional comfort from a male."

Karen said, "That would be fine."

Their comfort level grew and they had become good friends, at least in Karen's eyes. Then Carl put a stop to the physical contact. When she cried he wouldn't hug her.

The next session Karen asked, "Carl would you sit by me?"

"I'm just getting over a virus and I don't want you to get sick, Karen."

As the weeks without physical contact continued, Karen felt increasingly rejected, not only by her ex-husband but by her psychologist as well. Her anxiety and depression were full blown again. She was feeling more abandoned than she'd felt after her divorce. She couldn't stop crying and found it difficult to complete even the smallest of tasks. She felt hopeless and helpless.

"Carl, why don't you want to have contact with me anymore?"

"I don't feel it's healthy considering your fragile state, Karen."

Carl watched as Karen spiraled downward into more serious depression.

The needier she became, the more titillating Carl found the thought that such a woman would be so desperate for his affection. He was a balding older man that women of Karen's class rarely even noticed. He drew a sharp satisfaction from the extent of his control over Karen.

"Karen, if you wear that sheer pink blouse, I'll give you a hug," he said at their next session. She complied without hesitation.

"Karen, if you don't wear your bra for the next session, I'll give you a back massage," he whispered. Karen agreed, and kept on agreeing to Carl's requests. In return she received small gestures of physical attention.

Karen started talking about her controlling, authoritarian father in therapy sessions. She told Carl her father never paid any attention to her and was mentally abusive to her and her mother. She also talked about her mother's inadequacies and said she felt she had inherited many of them. Carl listened intently. At the end of the session he said, "If you wear my favorite low cut blouse and a short skirt to our next session, I'll kiss you."

Karen was elated and came to the therapy session dressed as per Carl's request. She spent much of the time anticipating that kiss.

"Karen, you're wearing the wrong blouse," Carl said as the session drew to a close.

"What?"

"You must have misunderstood. I wanted you to wear the sheer blouse. I'm not interested in kissing you—you didn't do as I asked."

Karen started crying—loud. Carl's next client was in the waiting room.

"Karen, if you stop crying now, I'll take you out for dinner tonight."

"I'd love that."

Carl met Karen at one of the most extravagant restaurants in New York City. Karen looked amazing in her low cut black dress, her long black wavy hair flowing over her shoulders. Carl smiled to himself when heads in the restaurant turned to look at her as the two of them walked to their table.

Carl had never been with such a beautiful woman. They sat in the corner of the restaurant, drinking wine and holding hands. They even kissed a couple of times, long romantic kisses that Karen responded to enthusiastically. Carl was so busy staring at Karen he didn't notice William, the psychologist with whom Carl shared his downtown office, sitting a few tables away with his wife, Constance.

Constance said, "Bill, that looks like Carl—that's not his wife, is it?"

Bill sighed. "I think it's a patient. I recognize her."

"But isn't that unethical?" she said.

The next morning William called the American Psychological Association to file a complaint. Following an investigation, Carl lost his license and his practice.

When Karen arrived home that evening the house was dark. As she walked by the living room she heard Carl's voice.

"Where were you this evening? I've been calling you, but you must have decided not to answer my phone calls."

Karen stared at Carl in the dark living room. The shadows across his face made him look older. He was wearing blue sweat pants and a t-shirt and his stomach was bigger than ever. His hair had markedly receded from the days when Karen had seen him for therapy.

"I was at the grocery store," she said.

"Do you think it's an appropriate signal, wearing something like that to the store?"

"It's just a shirt, Carl, and I told you where I was." She headed upstairs.

"Don't you ever walk away from me!" he said in a loud sharp voice.

Karen stopped in her tracks.

"You were at Jen's house, weren't you? You know I don't like you spending time with her, she fills you up with bullshit about our relationship."

As Karen looked at Carl, a wave of sadness came over her.

"How do you know I was with Jen? Let me see, was it my computer you were going through, or was it my cell phone? Or maybe it was the private detective you have following me."

Carl's voice turned somber. "You're becoming paranoid again," he said. "Remember the last time this happened? You had to go to the inpatient psychiatric unit for months."

"That was two years ago, Carl."

"You could be relapsing."

Was she being paranoid? Was Carl looking out for her best interests? He walked over to Karen and gave her a huge hug.

"Honey, why you don't go upstairs and draw yourself a bath? I'll bring you a Valium. Once you calm down things will look clearer. I'm suspending your driving privileges until you feel better—I'd hate to see you get in an accident."

Karen did as she was told, but when Carl brought the Valium, she pretended to take it, then spit it out in the sink as soon as he was out of sight.

That night, as soon as she heard Carl snoring, she got out of bed, put her clothes on, then snuck downstairs. Every creak down the staircase seemed as loud as a gunshot. When she got to the bottom, she walked outside into the crisp cold air and hailed a cab. Only then did she dare to look back.

Karen never saw Carl again outside a courtroom. Almost immediately after her separation from him, she began what turned out to be a swift recovery from her psychological issues.

Karen's Meeting:

Karen had just moved back to Saint Paul, Minnesota, when she came into my office. She said she was from upstate New York, but her mother lived here and she needed a place for the time being. She was a very attractive woman who had a difficult time making eye contact.

She said she'd been through some tough years and needed someone to talk to.

"I picked you because of your website," she said. "I wanted to see a doctor of psychology who was a woman. I didn't do so well with my last therapist. Then I saw that you worked with prisoners, and I thought that anyone who can work with prisoners wouldn't be so judgmental. I have a hard time with people judging me."

"That's fair," I said. "You don't need to be judged. If I were to judge you, then I'd be projecting my own issues onto you, and if I was doing that I should go back to school to learn how to be a non-judgmental therapist."

Karen seemed to relax a little.

"Do you want to talk about the therapist that didn't work for you?"

"I have a hard time trusting right now, because he was such a controlling and manipulating man," Karen said. "Someday I might tell you the story."

Karen's Background:

Karen filled out a consent form, so I was able to obtain her previous psychological testing and diagnosis from her psychologist in New York. It turned out Dr. Carl Schimt was no longer practicing, but the receptionist at the large psychological offices in New York sent over the assessment material I requested.

Considering the number of sessions, the notes I expected to see in Karen's files were missing, skimpy, or incomplete. Carl's notes documented a patient who was far more psychologically distraught than Karen actually seemed. It was apparent from the notes alone that he'd used his professional findings to take advantage of his patient's vulnerabilities.

When I spoke to his colleague, William, I learned the whole story. Carl had indeed used his therapeutic power illegally, losing his wife and practice, everything he had—except for Karen, whom he kept for several years through deception and manipulation.

Unfortunately, some therapists and psychologists do have affairs with their clients. Statistically, these affairs occur more frequently with middle-aged male therapists and female clients at least ten years their junior. The ramifications from the American Psychological Association are clear and severe for the therapist or psychologist who has an affair with a client or even makes sexual overtures.

Sexual touching from a therapist is *not* ethical. Sex with a therapy patient is unethical. And the harm to the patient can be devastating.

A therapist cannot have sex with an ex-client until the therapeutic relationship has been terminated for two years or more. Wanting to have sex with a client is not a reason for a therapist to terminate therapy. It should also be noted that if a therapist has had sex with an individual in the past, it is unethical for them to engage in a therapeutic relationship.

Karen's Recommendations:

1. Karen needs learn how to trust in herself.
2. She needs to work on her self-esteem issues.

3. She needs to practice making decisions on her own.
4. She needs assume responsibility for most major areas of her life.
5. Karen needs to make sure she is not vulnerable to men such as Carl in the future.
6. Karen needs to make everyday decisions with out excessive reassurance from others.
7. She needs to work through her issues with her father in therapy.
8. Karen needs to abstain from a partnership until she feels more comfortable with her judgment.
9. Karen needs to learn how to say no to unpleasant people or activities.
10. She needs to find a hobby or activity that she enjoys.

Although Carl refused to seek treatment at this time, typical recommendations for the puppeteer cheater may be like those below.

Carl's Recommendations:

- Carl needs to seek counseling for his control issues.
- He needs to establish proper boundaries in his life and work.
- Carl needs to acknowledge the harm he has inflicted on a therapy patient.

- He would benefit from group therapy to see how his actions affect others.
- He needs to come to terms with his abuse and disrespect to Karen.
- Psychotherapy is recommended to work on his childhood issues.
- Carl has to come to terms with the fact that his unethical actions have caused him to lose his career.

Tools: Are you a Puppeteer Cheater?

1. Do you find yourself putting down your partner to make yourself feel better?
2. Do you criticize your partner more than you should?
3. Do you make most of the decisions when you and your partner are together? Do you often refuse to let your partner make his/her own decisions?
4. Do you believe your partner isn't as smart or competent as you are?
5. Do you have very little respect for your partner?
6. Do you often treat your partner like a child or a teenager? Do you feel/behave as if you're the parent or older sibling in the relationship?
7. Do you feel you need to be in control at all times?

8. Do you make all the big money decisions without your partner's input?
9. If your partner does make a decision, do you fail to respect it? If he/she takes over a project, do you expect it to be screwed up?
10. Do you pursue sex outside your committed relationship with partners you can control?

If you said yes to five or more of the above questions chances are you're a Puppeteer Cheater and if your partner isn't letting you exert enough control, you'll find someone who will.

Note from Dr. Wood:

While many partners may not be as controlling as Carl, there are often controlling partners that may still be emotionally and/or physically abusive in the relationship. If you are in a relationship where you feel you are being controlled through mental or physical abuse, please seek the help of a therapist or other professionals, at once.

15

SOCIOPATHIC CHEATER
MALE

Hank

"You're sweating, Congressman. Drink, Sir?"

"Manhattan. Neat."

Representative of the State of Nebraska, Hank Manfred, was in the back of a limousine with a hat and dark glasses on at 11:30 on a Saturday night. Two of his most trusted bodyguards, Burt and Tony, stared motionless at the dark streets. They wore professional poker faces and pretended not to know where the Congressman was going, but they knew. They were going to the Congressman's regular Saturday night haunt, a private club called The Washington Dungeon.

Jerry, an obnoxious ruddy-faced lobbyist for the tobacco industry, provided the limo and rode along.

Jerry handed him the drink the way Hank liked it. "Let's not talk about that bill to help out tobacco not going through, Hank. Sure, tobacco folks aren't happy about it, but we all have setbacks and you did your best, right?"

"I did," Hank reassured him.

"We know you did. Besides a guy has to let his hair down sometimes, right? All work and no play, makes congressmen very boring. I should know. I've watched them at play for years now," Jerry said.

"Thanks."

Hank looked nervous and dripped sweat. His hands were shaking as they drove up the long drive to the private house, he popped a pill to calm himself.

Inside, Hank was in knots. His guts churned in mass confusion of anticipation, arousal, and fear. He had a hint of self-loathing, —but not enough to stop himself.

He quivered at the thought of his Mistress. Mistress Greta was the most beautiful and the most expensive dominatrix in the business. She ran the club.

Mistress Greta was said to inflict the most pain. Her cruel reputation made her the most desirable of mistresses and difficult to get an appointment with her.

Hank began his political career as the mayor who fought hard against crime in Omaha, he was known as the mayor that cleaned up the streets of prostitutes. The speeches on it became a popular platform when he ran as a Representative in Nebraska. His party platform echoed his promise to fight crime and put criminals behind bars where they belonged and the support of family values.

On Saturday nights and some weeknights, Hank was a hypocrite who supported dungeons and brothels, from the proceeds of generous special interest groups.

Hank would remind you of a flighty gazelle. He is bald with very white skin and thin eyebrows that hover on his round gray eyes. He has a week chin that sometimes gets lost in his shirt collar when his mouth is open, and he wears expensive suits that are compliments from special interest groups.

Hank kept his head low in case anyone on the street would recognize him in the stretch black bulletproof Mercedes as it cornered the streets of our nation's capital.

Hank couldn't get in to see Greta when he wanted to. It was Jerry that would pull the strings to set him up with the Mistress. Jerry would hand him cash to get into the club and do other favors that lobbyists do in D.C. to earn favor with their representatives. For example, escort Hank to the outings and wait for him, so Hank felt safe with Jerry watching his back.

Hank was a sex addict. When he couldn't get in to see Greta, other prostitutes would do. But his time with Mistress Greta he would play over and over in his head as his favorite time—as opposed to his time with his wife, Lorraine—which was never memorable.

Lorraine thought Hank suffered from Erectile Dysfunction and therefore was the dutiful wife who never brought it up again. She spent her time raising their three children and being responsible to their public image and personae. She went to church, volunteered for committees, would respond to some of Hank's correspondence for him, met with other wives of politicians, and would host Hank's social affairs.

Hank was rather proud of his secret sexual life. His time away from the marriage was totally under the radar. He would tell Lorraine that he was meeting with special interest groups and she would accept his words. Everyone around him was watching his back for him.

If they weren't, his escapades and spending would be a criminal act and he would lose everything—his career, position, power, and marriage. So although Hank had a lot riding on the secret being maintained, he had gotten away with it so long, he never even thought about what would happen if his secret became public.

Seeing Greta was like being tied to a bungee chord with a big drop. Only the ground is so far away, you could never see the ground. But however far the fall was, Hank knew one thing for sure. That it was going to hurt. It was going to hurt a lot. And he smiled.

"Got everything you need?" Jerry asked.

Hank felt a fat envelop in his inside breast pocket, "Yes, I'm set." He felt the $40,000 cash payout he had taken from Jerry after dinner.

"We'll be right here, Sir," Tony assured him.

"Thank you, yes, thank you." He knocked on the thick massive wood back door with the small peep door. It was set up for celebrities who didn't want to be seen entering the Washington Dungeon.

The peep door opened.

"Mr. Blue. I'm Mr. Blue," Hank was squirming in his suit he was so excited.

"Yes, Mr. Blue, is there more?"

"There's a calm before the storm."

The peep door closed and the big door opened for him. It felt so exclusive. Of all the privileges he had as a Congressman, this one felt the most powerful.

A man dressed as a London executioner was at

the door. He wore a black hood and tight swim trunks around a muscular 350-pound body.

"Mr. Blue, Mistress Greta says you are late."

"No, I'm right on time, our appointment was for midnight."

Hank heard a whip crack down the hall and he jumped when he recognized it.

"Snap!" the whip was getting closer. Mistress Greta had incredible mastery over the whip. She could make it tickle, or burn and cut. And those distinct sounds made her subjects associate the sound with a session with Mistress Greta. Greta knew this and used it to manipulate and heighten her clients' experience.

Mistress Greta appeared in the doorway. Hank could hardly breath he was so excited. He trembled and shook at Greta's presence remembering their last ordeal.

Mistress Greta was beautiful with long raven black hair to her waist with cool piercing light blue eyes.

She wore a black leather cat suit with a deep V-cut to her waist. She had a bountiful bust line that spilled out of her bustier part of her suit to her incredibly small waist. She had flaming red lips, and long, lean legs. She carried a long whip and small flogging crop that she would snap often near him.

"You have something for me?"

"Yes. How much?"

"$30,000 what you asked for, plus 10,000 for a tip."

"This is nothing. Don't look at me. You are not worthy to look at me."

She tied a strip of black leather blindfold over his eyes.

"I want to see where the rest of the money is," she said.

Hank Manfred laid spread-eagle in chains on the table.

She flogged him and snapped her whip near him. Sometimes she would make her whip caress his skin leaving a slight sting.

"I can get bigger fish than you, I throw away Presidents & Kings," she boasted as she continued her session.

That week the House of Representatives were surprised when Hank presented a new bill that would provide the tobacco industry tax relief on their best year ever. But the bill that meant millions to his lobby group didn't pass and Jerry thought Hank didn't do his job to line-up the support like he should have. Nothing was actually said to Hank and Hank assumed that it would be okay—they would try again later.

Hank was still comfortable that Jerry knew his secret sexual addiction and would keep it a secret for him. But things had changed last week when Hank didn't get the bill through. The tobacco industry had been paying for Hank's private life without any pay off, so Jerry set up Hank Manfred for the fall about to wipe out Hank Manfred's career.

When the uniformed cops first broke into Greta's, Hank thought they were part of the role-playing and were there to watch. But as he listened to them, as they pulled out real handcuffs, Hank realized they were real cops.

Three DC Police officers started snapping shots of the Congressman.

Flash! Flash! Flash! Flash!

"Stop the camera. No pictures!" Hank screamed.

Flash! Flash!

"No, please, no! Don't!"

Hank Manfred, you're under arrest for the solicitation of a prostitute."

"This is purely consensual," he spoke mildly and without urgency. Mistress Greta released Hank from the shackles for the cops. She set down the $40,000 envelop for them.

"Wait, this is a joke, right?"

"Congressman, you are really under arrest. We are Washington Police Officers and you will be booked with serious charges for your patronage here. Where did you get this $40,000 in cash, Congressman?"

Hank screamed. "Get Jerry. Find Jerry. He'll help me."

"Jerry got an urgent call and had to go, he told me to tell you, sorry," Greta said.

In that instant Hank had a powerful flash of realization. He had risked his position, future, prestige, career, and marriage—everything for this event.

He tried to look up but his head was shoved into the pillow and the officers were pushing him down to cuff him. He felt handcuffs go around his wrists, he struggled to get up, but the weight was far too heavy.

He heard "Mr. Congressman, you have the right to remain silent." He was read his Miranda rights and hauled out of the dungeon.

"No! Stop, no! I'm a Congressman for God's sake!"
Hank screamed again and again, as he was led away in handcuffs.

Hank was in shock as he was taken to the police car. He mumbled, "Call my attorney, someone call Fenster, Jacob Fenster."

Jerry got the camera back from the cop after the ordeal. In moments he E-mailed them to a contact that set them to music and uploaded the pictures to UPI, API, You Tube and other news websites. By morning the politician's career would be ruined by the unforgettable images posted and viewed by more than a million people after making the news channels.

Jerry approached Mistress Greta.

"Thanks, Greta." Jerry said. "You make Yale Drama School proud." Jerry handed her an envelop of cash.

"You'll get that bill through yet, Jerry," she said.

"I know."

Hank's Meeting

I was in my office at the Federal Correctional Facility when I heard the phone ring. I looked up at a clock wrapped in a protective steel grid. It was 4:00 and I thought it must be the intake unit, —more offenders were expected today.

"Hey, doc, this is Officer Martin from intake, we have a live one for you. It's some political bigwig. He's bawling like a little girl who got her doll run over."

"I heard someone else was coming, but they didn't tell me anything about him," I said.

"He is suicidal, Denise," Martin said. "I had to separate him from the rest of the offenders because they're picking on him."

"He said he wants to kill himself because his life is ruined and he is scared the prisoners will rape him, which they might if he doesn't quit crying like a baby."

"I'll see you in a few minutes," I said.

"Thanks, doc."

As I walked down the long corridor to the intake unit, I could hear my high heel shoes clicking all the way to the intake office. It was not unusual for offenders to be suicidal their first time in prison. They are often fearful that they will be killed, raped, or injured; which are all real possibilities.

I knocked on the door of the intake unit and Officer Johnson opened the door. "The nurses are done with Offender Manfred you can see him in the side office, here is his chart," said Officer Johnson.

I looked at the police report, no wonder he was terrified his whole life was turned upside-down.

I walked into the side office to see a man in an orange jumpsuit crying with his head buried in his hands. Mr. Manfred slowly looked up as I walked into the room. I had seen him on television a hundred times. He was a well-respected Congressman.

He looked so much smaller in person. His face was puffy and his eyes were bloodshot from crying, his white hair was disheveled. He looked similar to the other inmates.

He did not present the confident air that I had seen when I had watched him on television.

"Please, relax, Mr. Manfred. I have to ask you a few questions, "Are you suicidal, homicidal, or self-injurious?"

"Not homicidal," he said as he bit his lip hard enough to almost draw blood.

After assessing the Congressman for over an hour he was placed in solitary confinement.

As I walked back I heard my heels clicking down the empty corridor again. It was chow time so all of the offenders were eating. Shift change had just occurred with the officers, so they were busy with their shift change meeting.

I walked into the segregation unit. "Hey, doc, what brings you here this time of day?"

"I have a suicidal offender, his name is Mr. Manfred. I want no sharps, no amenities, bag lunch, and a tear resistant gown," I said.

"I also need him on fifteen-minute checks. Sorry, guys." I knew the officers hated the fifteen-minute checks, as they were redundant and time-consuming actions.

"I will drop off the paper work on my way out and be here tomorrow to assess Mr. Manfred for suicidal ideation."

As I walked out of the segregation unit I heard one of the offenders chanting, a threat to Manfred.

Hank's Background:

Sadly sex addicts and sex offenders are often victims of sexual abuse themselves.

It turns out that Mr. Manfred was a victim of abuse from the age of two. According to court documents Mr. Manfred and his mother had no place to live when Mr. Manfred's father passed away. Mrs. Manfred had no money, so she and her son went to live with Lyle Manfred, her brother-in-law, as his housekeeper.

Hank Manfred's mother stated in court that she walked into Lyle's room and found him sexually abusing Hank as a young child. However, she said nothing because she didn't think her son would remember the incident and she had nowhere else to go.

According to the reports Mr. Manfred was abused until the age of eight. Years later Mr. Manfred reported that he never wanted to be a victim again, and he wanted to control his surroundings in everyway possible. Politics were where he shined and he thought that he could control the political world.

With increased control Mr. Manfred admitted that he would then become aroused when he was controlled. Ms. Greta was one of the only people that he found had the ability to control him, which gave him great sexual satisfaction.

In addition, he stated that he became aroused by the thought of taking government money and spending it on his own deviant encounters he said that it gave him more power to think that the American people were suckers.

He admitted that he became cocky after getting away with this deviant behavior. The more he got away with this behavior, the more he wanted to continue to escalate the behavior. He said it was like an endorphin high that he could not get enough of. He admitted that if he had not been caught, he would still be seeing Ms. Greta.

Hank's Assessment

Hank began with an affair with a political aid and then escalated to hookers and other professionals. To keep his sexual addiction going, Hank accepted bribes from special interest groups. Being bought in Washington translates to low moral ethics and a lackluster career when rumors about his reputation became Washington gossip.

Hank's sexual addiction objectifies sex. In his case, hookers, his dominatrix, the thrill, the self-defeating aspect, all show lack of his own self-esteem. He tries to forget what a sell-out he is in his career and what a poor leader he is for his state.

His narcissist qualities and position hold him above the law. He thinks that no one is watching him enter. In fact the limo driver, Jerry, guys in the car, employees at the Club, lobbyists who fund his sexual trysts, etc. All know what he is doing. But he thinks himself so important they would guard his secret.

Hank no longer needs to really get off and be satisfied

sexually, he is coming to a place to humiliate himself and perhaps Greta is the only one that does not bow to his political position.

Instead she lowers him to verbal and physical abuse of what he may think, in fact, *deserves* for his acceptance of political bribes and "poor excuse for a Congressman" work ethics.

Sociopathic cheaters often keep escalating their sexual tendencies when they see they are not getting caught. They think they are above the law and will never get caught; so they feel a strong sense of gratification with getting away with acts against societal norms. Because they think that they are smarter than others, they assume they will get away with it.

Hank's Recommendations:

- Mr. Manfred needs to attend a sex offender program.
- He needs to assess his strengths and work with his weaknesses.
- Mr. Manfred needs to work through his abuse as a child.
- He needs to know that the weakness he felt is part of his past not his future.
- He needs to learn how to establish loving relationships.
- He needs to learn to relinquish control.
- Mr. Manfred needs to realize that he is not above the law.

- Mr. Manfred needs to be aware of how his deviant actions affect others not only himself.
- Mr. Manfred has to assess his need to act in anti-authoritative manner.

Tools: Are You a Sociopathic Cheater?

1. Do you fail to conform to society's norms, performing sexual acts that could get you/ your mate arrested? For example, Mr. Manfred and the prostitutes.
2. Do you con other people on a regular basis for personal profit or personal gain? For example, Mr. Manfred conning the system to make money for his sexual liaisons.
3. Do you find that you are very sexually impulsive? If a woman/man is making advances toward you sexually, do you instinctively have sex with her/him regardless of the consequences?
4. Most of the time do you find yourself disregarding your own personal safety? For example: You wear no condom when having sex with a woman/man you just met?
5. Are you often physically aggressive during sex even though your mate does not want to be? For example, Mr. Manfred's need for sexually aggressive tirades.
6. Have you discovered that you lack remorse after cheating on your mate? For example,

Mr. Manfred was only remorseful when he got caught.

7. Do you find that you lie or use a fake name, location, etc. to get sex? For example, Mr. Manfred used a fake name to obtain sex from Mistress Greta.

8. Do you find that even if you can't afford it, you are using money to obtain sex or enjoy sexual activities?

9. Have you physically hurt someone unintentionally while having sex?

10. Have you been arrested due to illegal sexual activity?

If you answered yes to five or more of the questions, you may be having problems maintaining a relationship because you have some of the tendencies of a Sociopathic cheater.

16

THE DEPENDANT CHEATER
FEMALE

Maggie

"Come here, Honey," Ben encouraged Maggie down a wooded path.

Maggie was so excited that her adventurous man was escorting her on this once in a lifetime experience.

She inhaled the fresh spring air and breeze from the lake and was charmed by the magical world of William Wordsworth's cottage. It was simply beyond exquisite.

Ben had snuck down to the lake early in the morning and had placed flowers in the boat along with a book of poetry. They both got in the boat and Ben started rowing. His broad shoulders were flexing with each row of the boat.

"Maggie, Maggie," Ben said.
"What?"
"You are daydreaming again," he said.

"Was I?" asked Maggie.
Maggie awakened to see Ben seated next to her in

the van. It was Saturday afternoon and this was Maggie and Ben's usual Saturday drive to the grocery store. Maggie knew the grocery list by heart because Ben was a meat and potatoes man that would only eat a few dishes that Maggie cooked.

"I refuse to eat anything that lives in the sea," Ben would say. Not that Ben had ever been to the sea, he rarely went anywhere out of their hometown.

"Let's rent a Vin Diesel movie," Ben said to Maggie.

"We've seen them all," she said.

"Yeah, but they're good again and again," he told her.

Maggie opened the window on Ben's van to get some fresh air into her lungs.

"Close the window, I've got the air on," he said.

She felt like she was suffocating—and it had nothing to do with the air.

Maggie had been dating Ben for three years. Every Saturday evening was the same plan. Ben would take her to the Old Country Buffet, where he would stack his plate with meat and potatoes.

They went to Red Box to rent 2 movies at .99 cents each.

At the buffet Ben would usually knock politics, religion, and celebrity and sports figures with the same irreverence.

"That scientology thing—that's a cult or something. Look at that Tom Cruise and his wife," Ben said. "They are not right."

After church Ben would get on the Internet and look

at the different guns online. He would show Maggie all of the different guns that he would like to put in his gun collection someday, when they made more money. Maggie would rather spend savings on her dreams—a trip to Europe and exotic adventures.

On one hand Maggie never felt insecure, Ben was stable, reliable, made a good salary, and was true to her. He wanted to marry Maggie, to have a family, and grow old with her. But he would never offer her the excitement that she craved. Ben was boring with no sense of adventure.

Maggie stared at the ceiling that night while Ben was thrusting himself inside her. They were in the missionary position, which was Ben's expertise—and only position.

"Shall we do it in the living room?" Maggie had asked before they started.

"What are we, kids? We got a bed. Why would we do that?" he asked. "Sex between a man and a woman takes place in the bedroom."

Ben was grunting as he thrust deeper inside Maggie and Maggie knew Ben was about to climax. After he did, he rolled over and started snoring immediately.

Maggie had only been with Ben. She never had experimented with herself, never had another man—and never had an orgasm. The women at bridal showers would talk about orgasms, but Maggie had no idea what an orgasm felt like.

One morning after Ben left for work, Maggie took some extra time on her hair and makeup and stopped by Caribou Coffee on the way to work. She saw a handsome man at a table and picked the empty table near him.

He glanced at Maggie with a look that sent a jolt of electricity in her being as she sat down.

"You are not from around here are you?" Maggie smiled.

"No. I'm Marcus Mackenzie from Scotland."

"I'm Maggie," she said

"My first love was an Irish girl named Maggie," he said.

"Was she good to you?" Maggie asked.

"Well, that is a long story, maybe I should tell you about it over dinner," he said as his eyes looked deeply into hers. "Do you know of any nice places to eat around here?"

"Why yes I do," said Maggie with a grin.

"Would you join me?" he asked.

She thought a moment. Tonight was Ben's bowling night, so Maggie would be safe until at least 11 pm.

"I'll meet you at a restaurant downtown called Faux Le Duet. Can you find it?" she asked.

"I'm sure I can. Shall we say 7:30?" he asked.

"Yes, I would love that," she said.

Maggie's Meeting:

Maggie was an average looking woman in every way with the exception that she had vibrant red hair. She looked a bit disheveled when she entered my office that Monday afternoon.

"How is this week going Maggie?" She avoided eye contact and fidgeted while she spoke.

"I had a really hard week," she said. "I told Ben about my date with the foreign guy."

"How did he react?" I asked.

"Ben told me to get my stuff and get out. I begged him not to break up with me. I said that I would kill myself if he left me," she began to sob.

"Are you suicidal?" I asked.

"Yes," she said with tears streaming down her face.

"Do you have a plan?" I asked.

"Yes. I've been hoarding pills. I am going to take some pills," she said softly.

"Maggie I need to call your parents right away and they have to take you to the psychiatric unit in the hospital. Do you understand?"

She shook her head yes.

I had my receptionist cancel my next two appointments and waited with Maggie until her parents arrived.

"I called the Fairview Riverside psychiatric unit and they are expecting Maggie. Maggie will be placed on a seventy-two hour hold. They will assess her after that. I will call to see how she is doing later on today."

Maggie's parents just nodded. I could tell by the looks on their faces that they were terrified.

Maggie's Background:

Maggie was an obedient child. She did as she was told and never went through a rebellious time as a teenager.

Her parents thought she was the easiest of their three children to raise. Maggie was the oldest and never needed to be told twice to do any of their wishes.

She stayed away from sports, enjoyed spending time alone reading in the library. She would often meet men in the library or daydream about certain frequent visitors to the library. Coffee houses were nice too.

She loved to dream away the day with the chance, that her knight would see her while buying his daily coffee. When that didn't happen she would go watch her soap operas that she had taped on Tivo—and she could fill hours every night, watching her favorite soap operas.

When Maggie got her first serious boyfriend, she went straight from her parent's house to her boyfriend's house. She never lived alone and never paid a bill on her own. She liked it that way. When a relationship turns bad, Maggie stays in it and tries not to change the status quo. If she decided to leave the sinking ship, it would mean moving, looking for another man, which is way too much work.

She can just dream about it being another way in her head. And often if she dreams it enough, she'll meet him, and then it all works out.

Maggie's Assessment:

The notes I received from Maggie's last doctor stated that Maggie needed extensive advice and assurance from others. He identified her as a dependent personality.

Maggie is very passive in her presentation. She allows her significant other to assume responsibility for most major decisions in her life. She often stays in relationships were she is unhappy because she fears being alone. She does not believe that she has the ability to take care of herself.

Maggie lacks self-confidence and believes that her boyfriend, Ben can do things better than she can—so she never initiates anything. Maggie lets her significant other, Ben, call all the shots and make all the decisions in their relationship.

Her whole life revolves around what Ben wants to do. Although this is the life that Maggie has chosen, she has become bitter toward Ben as she feels that he is not romantic enough—and boring. Bored in the relationship she dreams about a fantasy world.

She prefers to live in a fantasy world, where she mentally dissociates so she does not have to deal with the reality of her existence. She acknowledges she feels stuck in a boring life and that she craves excitement and more in life.

Maggie's Recommendations:

- Maggie needs to be placed on a 72-hour hold because she is suicidal and she does have a plan.
- Maggie should not be released from the hospital until she denies suicidal ideation.
- When Maggie is released she needs to see a therapist on a weekly basis.
- Maggie would benefit from assertiveness training in therapy.
- Maggie should establish her own hobbies.

- She needs to establish more self-confidence through Cognitive Behavioral Therapy.
- She would benefit from group therapy.
- Maggie needs to establish a support system other than her parents and significant other.
- Maggie needs to be assessed for anti-depressants.
- She needs to become educated on her sexual desires with a sex therapist.

Tools: Are you a Dependent Cheater?

1. Do you do everything your significant other does and ignore your own needs?
2. Is it difficult for you to make a decision without your mate?
3. If you know that one relationship is ending do you start looking for another relationship?
4. Does your heart start racing if you think of yourself without a partner?
5. Do you feel like you don't really love your mate, but you don't want to be alone?
6. Have you said that you will kill yourself if your significant other stated that they want to leave you?
7. Do you lack self-esteem if you do not have a significant other?

If you answered yes to four or more of the questions stated above you maybe a Dependent Cheater.

SITUATIONAL

CHEATERS

TYPES OF CHEATERS

Situational Cheaters comprise the second group of cheaters. In general, these cheaters have an easier time in treatment, which often is shorter in duration and not as involved as with the Personality Cheaters. Situational cheaters have the best prognosis for becoming monogamous again—or for the first time in their relationships.

Situational cheaters tend to be more remorseful in their initial therapy sessions. They may cheat because they're trying to compensate for a difficult patch in their life, or trying to fill a painful void, or looking for the ideal mate to save them from their misery.

Once situational cheaters have accepted an understanding of why they cheated, they can save themselves. By attending therapy sessions, they can learn how to cope with the pain they caused. Situational cheaters tend to be willing to work out their problems with their partners and move on, leaving the past behind them.

Abandoned Cheater

The Abandoned Cheater usually suffered a major personal loss, such as the death of a loved one, the termination of an important relationship, the infidelity of a partner, the failure of a career. Abandoned cheaters often suffer from depression and may seek emotional and physical comfort from others. These cheaters may feel as if their partners don't understand them.

They may go from sexual encounter to sexual encounter seeking solace of some sort. They may realize their sexual encounters aren't taking their emotional pain away, become even more depressed, and seek therapeutic guidance.

Once they feel stable they're more likely to develop coping skills that can be used the next time they have to deal with a traumatic experience. If they've achieved an understanding of their bereavement issue, they're less likely to cheat again.

Revenge Cheater

The Revenge Cheater has suffered the infidelity of a partner and has low self-esteem issues. Feeling hurt and attacked from their cheating partner, they have a primitive reaction to attack and hurt back. They believe that their act of cheating will help them feel better, but it is not satisfying—and they feel worse. The second act of infidelity also compounds the problems in their relationship.

The Revenge Cheater now faces the guilt from what they have done, creating a vicious cycle of abuse and guilt within the relationship. Detached and disengaged from their partnership, the Revenge Cheater may have a tendency to become depressed.

The act they are performing is for acceptance and love, and when the infidelity falls short, the cheater suffers again. The act of cheating for the Revenge Cheater is truly stepping out of their own personae to do an act that is not within their personality or character.

The act is meant to make them feel better and desirable, but instead the whole system becomes even more broken. The challenge will be for both partners to address their self-esteem issues, put their infidelity in the past, and move forward in the present.

Eternal Youth Cheater

The female Eternal Youth Cheater is often called a cougar, and certainly these women like to have power and control over their young "prey." This cheater typically looks and acts much younger than her real age.

The female eternal youth cheater feels a certain entitlement to get what she wants and will stop at nothing until she succeeds. This woman is often in a power position at work or has some sort of fame. The female eternal youth cheater usually has money and sees no reason not to date a younger man. Only when her husband or boyfriend discovers her infidelity will she seek therapy—if then. Once in therapy she learns how to deal with her pending issues of power and control over others.

The male eternal youth cheater will seek younger women so he can recapture the feeling of youth and omnipotence he experienced in his twenties. Predictably, this cheater is usually struggling with a mid-life crisis. He's not just frightened of getting older; he sees his own mortality dwindling rapidly. He thinks he has to have all the fun he can before he becomes elderly or sick.

He seeks comfort in the thought that younger women still find him attractive. His affairs give his self-esteem a superficial boost. Eternal youth cheaters typically won't seek therapy unless their partners catch them, if then.

Emotional Cheater

Emotional Cheaters are often unhappy with their partnership. They may feel ignored, or feel that their partner no longer cares what they have to say. Missing emotional compassion, they seek it from someone other than their partners.

Emotional cheaters don't cross the line of physical intimacy, so they don't think they're cheating and will deny infidelity if questioned.

They may cheat emotionally through letters or innocent meetings they find titillating because they know their partners wouldn't approve. They often emotionally cheat online or via e-mail or text messages and are great fans of Face book and Twitter. But for all this communication, emotional cheaters tend to lack the communication skills to tell their partners about their emotional needs. This is understandable, since without therapy these cheaters have trouble knowing what their actual needs and desires *are*—they're rarely in touch with their emotional needs. But once they become aware of their desires and needs and are able to communicate them to the partner, they rarely need to continue emotional cheating to fill the hole that drove them to seek out these relationships.

Quiet Cheater

Quiet Cheaters rarely express their unhappiness with their partners. They often look like half of a happy couple—or may have tried to rekindle the relationship with a partner, often with no response.

Quiet Cheaters commonly feel completely ignored by their partners. They may say they're still with the partner because they don't want to split up the assets or upset family members or friends. They may feel as if their partner is a stranger.

These cheaters often sleep separately from their partner. They rarely seek couples therapy or counseling. *What's the use? My partner will never change.*

Though they live together they often tell people they're separated, because that's how they feel. They may describe their relationship as hopeless and say they feel helpless about the prospect of strengthening it

Depressed about their relationship with their partners, these cheaters seek physical and emotional intimacy from someone they feel understands them. Often, when the quiet cheater enters a relationship that makes him/her happy, the partner becomes more attracted to the cheater, who no longer seems depressed.

This change in dynamics may send the couple into therapy, where they can try to work through their roadblock.

17

ABANDONED CHEATER
FEMALE

Maria

"It's been a week, Maria," Jose said. "You have other children who need you."

Maria was curled in a ball on the bed.

"Did you hear me?" he said. "I can't do it all by myself. The children need their mother."

Maria didn't move. Wouldn't speak.

"Damn it, you can't just hide here. We have to get on with life. I'm going to work. Make the kids their breakfast." He set a dollar bill on the dresser. "Miguel needs to bring a dollar to school for supplies for something. "

No movement.

"Maria, the world didn't stop because our baby was stillborn. Thank God for the three beautiful children we have—if you want another, we can try again. Te quiero, Maria. Please, please don't let me find you in bed again when I get home."

He left her. Alone. On her worst day since the birth. She couldn't believe God was so cruel to her. Her body was torn from the full-term pregnancy, her heart in pieces from the funeral with that tiny white casket. She got on her knees to pray to God, but all that came out was a wail from her depths to the universe. It was such a horrifying sound the children all came running into her bedroom.

"Mama, mama!" They stared at their tortured mother and didn't know how to help her. Finally the oldest, Roberto, said, "Mama, I'm here for you. We love you, Mama."

The hospital offered grief counseling, but she had no time to do it with three kids who needed her attention.

She would try to play with her children, but she'd see an infant and start to cry again. She grieved. Days passed. She hid her sorrow as best she could, because whenever Jose saw her look sad he said, "Time to get over it."

More days passed. Jose thought everything was back to normal. Maria kept pretending all was well and after six weeks went back to her job as a social worker. When Jose made love to her, she wasn't engaged. Sex reminded her of her loss—she wasn't sure why she felt that way, but she did.

Paulo, a good-looking new social worker, came on board at the office. Maria and Paulo began to eat lunch at the Penguin Pub, which had intimate booths in a quiet area of the restaurant.

"Maria, this is none of my business, but you seem like you need to talk," he said the third time they met. "If you ever need an ear, I want you to know I'm here for you."

She paused for a moment. Hard to believe the permission to talk about it was finally there.

"Paulo, I just lost my baby," she said.

The tears she knew were always behind her eyelids overflowed, and he rushed to her side and held her right there in the restaurant. Maria grabbed his strong shoulders, then went limp and cried uncontrollably in his arms.

"How could God have done this to you?" he said. "I'm so sorry for you. You're a beautiful woman, Maria, and I'm here for you. Cry, go ahead and cry. I'm not going anywhere—I'm here for you, cry as long as you want. Dear God, this is tragic." He continued holding her tightly and reassuring her that he was there for her, never trying to stem her emotional flood.

When she finally stopped crying she looked up and saw that the sweet man holding her while she sobbed had streams of tears coursing down his own face. He was crying with her.

"Oh, Paulo," she said.

She knew in that moment that she'd be breaking her marriage vows—and soon after that beautiful connection with Paulo, she did.

On Mondays and Wednesdays Paulo would leave the office on his lunch break, and soon Maria would join him. She walked through a restaurant to an alley where Paulo's car was waiting for her.

Paulo had the key to a buddy's apartment just a couple minutes away from work.

They snuck away to their love nest whenever they could.

But Paulo's wife, Juanita, became suspicious. She took a day off work, followed him one Monday morning, and went into the building just after Paulo and Maria. She pounded on the apartment door like a madwoman, and when Paolo answered she stormed into the room.

"Paulo, you cheating bag of scum!" she screamed. "I love you, what's the matter with you? You lose me for a tramp!"

"Juanita, I didn't mean for this to happen, it's just that she needed someone so—,"

he said.

"You think *I* don't need you?" Juanita screamed. She turned and glared at Maria. "Bitch, get your own husband!"

"I have one," Maria whispered.

"Paulo, this ends today." Juanita said.

"Yes, yes, of course," he said.

"You'll change jobs, we *will* be moving, or I leave and take the kids," she said.

"Okay, okay. You're right."

"Tramp, if you ever call my husband, text him, e-mail him, I'll come back with my knife. Got it?" Juanita shook a finger as she talked.

"I've got it," Maria said.

Maria tried to go deeper into her relationship with Jose, he seemed so cold after Paulo she couldn't really feel it. One Monday she went to the Penguin Pub. The host welcomed her warmly and seated her in a booth.

"Your friend? Will he be coming?"

"No," she said. "We're not seeing each other anymore."

"He must be crazy," he said, taking away the other table setting. "I'm Hector Alexandro, I own this restaurant."

"Maria Estevan."

"If you're alone today, may I join you? I'll have my chef make us something special."

"I would love that, Hector," Maria said.

She still managed to be a good mother to her children and was there whenever Jose needed her. But when she needed a shoulder to lean on, she'd learned to look elsewhere.

Before long Maria was having an affair with Hector, which lasted for a few months until she ended it for Daniel.

Maria's Meeting:

When Maria came into my office she seemed tired, sullen, and distraught. She said she and her family moved to Minneapolis from California after her husband lost his job. She said her husband's parents lived here, and they were living with them until Jose found work. She said she thought it was too cold in Minnesota and she was waiting to go back to California some day.

Maria talked about the pain she experienced when she lost her baby, then said she'd had several affairs since the baby died. She wasn't proud of her infidelities, but these men gave her the comfort Jose couldn't. "Being with them is the only thing I do that numbs the pain."

She said Jose was a good father, but she could never forgive him for not comforting her in her time of need.

She said sex with Jose was "cold," and she counted numbers in her head while he made love to her.

"I've gotten to five hundred twice," she said, looking down at the floor. She acknowledged that the affairs made her feel guilty but said she was unable to stop.

"They're the only thing I have to look forward to in life. After I have sex with one of the men I go straight to confession." She started to cry. "I believe I'll end up in hell for what I've done," she said when she calmed down. "But I live a hell on earth, so what's the difference? God is punishing me.

"Dr. Wood? Sometimes late at night I hear my baby crying out for his mommy, but I can't soothe him. He's far away—with God. Why did God take him from me?"

Maria's Background:

Maria was a beautiful child, adored by her large family and everyone around her. Her parents, Pedro and Bonita, were hardworking people who knew how to love, and the family was very close.

Pedro worked long hours in Mexico to provide for his six children. When Maria was just twelve, a construction accident left Pedro paralyzed. Since medical care in Mexico was substandard, her mother had to work long hours in addition to caring for Pedro. The construction company didn't help, and Bonita got little sleep as she tried valiantly to hold her family together for several years.

When family members insisted that Bonita attend a neighbor's wedding celebration, Pedro died at home, unattended for two hours. Bonita never forgave herself for abandoning her love—nor could she forgive God for taking him. She lost her faith, no longer believing in a merciful God. She spent years trying to get over the depression and guilt she felt for leaving Pedro.

Maria remembers trying to help her mother through her depression, throughout her teenage years. She herself was filled with love and praise for God. She was active in her Catholic church, and her faith and love were the most important things in her life.

Maria's Assessment:

Maria is suffering from feelings of hopelessness, worthlessness, and excruciating guilt. She has lost interest in all the activities she used to enjoy, particularly spending time with her family.

She has no appetite, is tired most of the day, and finds it hard to concentrate at work. She has confessed to suicidal thoughts but has no plan. She said she would never commit suicide because of her Catholic upbringing. "I don't need to add a mortal sin to everything else," she told me.

She said there are times when she wants to be with her dead baby. Since her symptoms were still apparent two months after the baby's death, Maria is most likely experiencing a major depressive single episode.

Maria made a deliberate, rational (to her) choice to ease her emotional void with affairs when she didn't get the support she needed from Jose after the stillbirth. Although she's well aware that a new liaison won't take her pain away, she always sees it as a temporary solution to her personal misery.

She feels that no one understands her pain yet she's found lovers who feel her loss with her. She thinks her husband is being cold and callous about her feelings and the loss of their baby. The fact that he may be hurting too and grieving in a different way hasn't occurred to her.

Instead of supporting each other during their mourning period, couples are more often driven apart by the loss of a child. Whether from guilt, blaming one another, or being unable to communicate effectively about the death, the couple may not come through this low point in their marriage together. They lose touch with their love for each other or don't give themselves permission to have fun again. Whatever the reason, the death of a child always signals a danger point for a marriage—no matter how solid it was before the loss.

Maria's Recommendations:

- Maria needs to attend a support group for people who've lost children through death or stillbirth. She will benefit from an ongoing support system.
- She needs individual counseling to help her grieve the death of her baby in ways that will assist in the healing process.
- Maria and Jose could benefit from couples counseling.
- Maria needs to be honest with Jose about the

affairs and about feeling betrayed when he kept trying to get her to "move on" after the stillbirth.

- She needs to understand that all individuals grieve differently and acknowledge Jose's pain. Jose needs to let Maria grieve at her own pace. They need to talk to each other about how the death has affected them, each listening carefully and avoiding all judgment.
- Maria needs to let go of the guilt while working through her grief.
- She should be assessed for an anti-depressant.
- Family therapy would be beneficial since the children sense the sadness and grief within the household and have feelings of their own they may need help sorting out.

Tools: Are You an Abandoned Cheater?

1. Have you lost someone you loved recently and feel that your partner has little or no sympathy for your loss?
2. Do you feel alone in your loss and seek solace from others who may have been through a similar situation or simply be more compassionate than your partner?
3. Do you find yourself attracted to people you think can take better care of your emotional needs than your partner? Does sex with them give you temporary release from your misery?

4. Do you feel your partner has let you down to the point that you're perpetually angry about it?
5. Do you feel your partner left you emotionally after a traumatic event or unexpected death?
6. Do you feel you have no one to turn after your loss, even though you have a partner who loves you?
7. Do you feel excessive guilt over the loss of your loved one?
8. Do you feel disconnected physically from your partner since the loss of your loved one? Mentally?
9. Do you feel disconnected from life after the loss of your loved one?

If you answered yes to four or more of these questions you may be an abandoned cheater.

18

ABANDONED CHEATER
MALE

Tom

Tom sat up and screamed. "NO!"

He'd been in a restless sleep. Now his heart was racing, and he gulped to catch his breath.

Jill rolled over and held him. "You're okay, Tom. I'm here."

"Go back to sleep, honey. I'm fine."

Tom grabbed his robe and walked downstairs. In the living room he sat in darkness. Why was he still having these nightmares? He hated to be awake because he never knew when his mind would relive it, and he didn't want to go back to sleep because he never knew when his mind would redream it.

He poured himself a scotch and sat in a leather chair and let the tormenting thoughts overtake his mind.

Fifteen years ago...

"Can I wear your bomber jacket?" Tom's brother, Tony, yelled from the other room.

"Sure, just don't get ketchup on it, you slob." Tom would do anything for his little brother. He was the gifted one: smart, athletic, accomplished, and handsome. Everyone wanted to hang out with Tony. Tom and Tony were a year apart, and Tony's popularity got Tom more dates.

"I can't be late for practice again, the coach will make me do extra drills."

"I'm coming," Tom yelled down the stairs.

"Tom, get your brother to hockey now!" his dad hollered.

"Maybe I should drive. I need practice," Tony said.

"I'm the designated driver, hot shot," Tom said.

Tom and Tony were both good-looking and athletic. Tom was seventeen, Tony sixteen. Everything seemed to come effortlessly for Tony, even girls. He had a contagious grin and a playful way about him that made him fun to be around. His attitude toward life was always positive and he seemed to know how to please the toughest of audiences—even their father lightened up when Tony was around. Tom may have been a bit jealous of Tony at times, but he and Tony were the closest of brothers and the best of friends.

"Dude, drive faster," Tony said.

"Hey, it's kind of icy—you know the curves here."

"Who taught you to drive—-Grandma?" Tony said. "Come on, there's no traffic."

Tom pulled around a sharp curve but punched the pedal a little—until he felt the car start to skid on a patch of black ice. He tried to correct, but none of the tires had a grip—they were all turned and the car was spinning right into the steep hill. *Well, that's okay. We can't get too hurt running into a dirt hill at a low speed.*

They came to a stop at the base of the hill. Tom threw the car into reverse to correct his path and continue to the hockey game.

At that moment a semi truck in the other lane rounded the curve; the driver saw the boys stalled in his lane, braked—and hit the black ice. He skidded right into the boys' car.

Tony said, "I love you."

When Tom awoke in the hospital, his mother and father standing over him.

"God, you guys look like shi—you look terrible," Tom said. "Am I dying?"

"No," his mom whispered.

"Where's Tony?"

"Tony is...he's gone." Tom's mother sounded a million miles away. She wasn't crying, looked like she was cried out. Tom couldn't cry, couldn't feel anything, couldn't remember what happened—he was in shock. He couldn't even imagine life without Tony.

The hospital stay was hard to recall, as Tom was in shock and on pain pills. He fell in and out of consciousness.

"NO!" Tom screamed when he remembered the semi skidding into them, "Not Tony, oh god, not Tony." He was struggling to get out of the hospital bed. His father was trying to hold him down.

"You can help me pack if you want to, I'll be staying with your aunt in Florida for a few weeks," his mom said.

Looked to Tom like she was taking everything she owned.

"You understand, don't you, Tom?"

"Sure," Tom said. "No problem."

"Do you hear your father and me fight at night?"

"I reckon the whole neighborhood hears," Tom said. He gave her an understanding smile.

"You look just like your brother when you smile," she said as she turned away from him.

"You're not coming back, are you?"

His mom denied it, but when she left that day he never saw her again. She eventually remarried and wrote that she was happy. Tom knew why: his mother had seen Tony every time she looked at him after the accident. He understood why she couldn't take it.

The house felt empty without his mom and Tony. Tom's dad numbed himself in his chair.

"A scotch neat is the best drink known to man," his father said from the dark living room. "Tom, sit down, I barely ever see you any more."

"Okay," Tom said.

"Can't hear you, did you answer me? If you're going to answer me, do it like a man."

"Okay."

"Your brother was a man, he'd know what I'm talking about. What would you know about being a real man? He could have gone pro. You know that, don't you?"

Tom walked over to his father's chair and loomed over him.

"Here's what I know, Dad. I know I wish it was me

who died in that accident every minute of every day. Just like you do."

That was the last time Tom ever spoke to his father. He moved in with his girlfriend Jill's parents and lived there until they finished high school. They went to the same college, got married, and moved into an apartment together.

Tom played college football and recalls seeing his father at one of his football games. His father was stumbling around in the bleachers, drunk and disheveled. Tom scored several points that day, glad his father wasn't among the crowd for the victory celebration.

Even fifteen years after the accident, Tom's memories of Tony were excruciatingly painful. He walked into the dark kitchen. His hands were shaking, his head was spinning, and his heart was pounding. He felt like he was going crazy. He started throwing pill bottles from the cupboard onto the floor. The room was spinning, and he couldn't stop it.

He fell to the floor, glass and pill bottles surrounding him. He found them. He took the Valium the doctor had prescribed for him and sat down in the glass shards. The tears kept streaming down his face. He looked up to see Jill staring at him, her face filled with horror. She ran up the stairs as fast as she could.

"Shit," said Tom as he sat in the darkness. His body had finally stopped shaking. He looked at the mess around him. His body felt weak. He was dizzy and had a throbbing headache and pain in his chest. It wasn't the first time he'd experienced this crushing loss of losing control.

The first time it happened he had Jill rush him to the hospital because he thought it was his heart. Turned out to be a full-fledged panic attack. He was given Ativan and told to see a psychologist for cognitive behavioral therapy. Tom never made an appointment.

The room was filled with darkness and Tom fell into a deep REM sleep on the couch. He woke up to find Jill standing over him.

"Oh, shit," he said, "I'm late for work." He sprang to his feet and gave Jill a huge kiss. "Have a good day," he said as he ran up the stairs. He jumped into the shower.

Tom's presentation was today. He always made a great impression on his clients, and he wasn't about to let them down now. His good looks and enthusiasm won over any audience, and his advertising firm landed the account.

"You did it again, boss," Neil said. "So when are we off to Vegas to celebrate and promote the campaign? I hope you're not leaving without me."

"Of course not," Tom said. "You're lucky in craps and a great wing man."

"You always seem to find someone to play with," Neil said.

Jill found Tom stirring on the couch when she got home from work.

"Must have fallen asleep," he said. "How long have you been standing there?"

"Long enough to know you're exhausted from last

night," Jill said. "I've asked you several times to get help. You know your problems aren't going to go away on their own. How long before you do something? For god's sake, it's been over fifteen years."

"Baby, you know I just go through some stuff every once in a while—everyone does, right?" Tom shot Jill one of his big grins, and she couldn't help but smile back. "Now I have to get moving. I have to go to Vegas in the morning."

"When are you going to be back?"

"I'll be home on Monday, do you think you can live without me that long?" Tom grinned and gave Jill a kiss on the cheek. "I love you so much."

Jill knew he meant it, but his demons where so overpowering. And though she was a devoted wife, she knew she could end up leaving Tom. His trips to Las Vegas no longer included her and were more frequent. At first he said it was to let off steam with a guy friend, then it became regular gambling trips. She checked their account, and he never seemed to lose money but he never seemed to come back with extra money either. Most troubling was the fact that there seemed to be less sex in the past year between them.

"Let's play some craps." Tom couldn't help but notice the two women on the other side of the table. "Buddy check out the chicks at three o'clock," he said to Neil.

Neil looked to his right and saw a beautiful brunette and a long-haired redhead. "Which one do you want?" Neil asked.

"I'll call the redhead," said Tom. He raised his arm.

"Waitress, please send two drinks over to the beautiful ladies at the other end of the table. My friend will have a beer, I'll have a scotch neat."

The foursome moved easily to the bar area and then to their respective hotel rooms.

"How adventuresome are you, Leah?" Tom asked.

"Like for travel?"

"How about in bed?" he said. "You're one of the sexiest women I've ever seen."

"Really?"

"Definitely," he said.

"Nobody's ever told me that before," she said.

"Well, darlin', the men in Wyoming must have too much dust in their eyes," he said.

"I can't believe you aren't married," she said. "You seem like the kind of guy some girl would have snapped up by now."

"Just you and me, Leah," he said. "Are you going to tease me all night? I want to make love to you."

"Well..." She looked like she was about to expound on why she shouldn't leave her friend, but Tom took her hand and turned to Neil and Elaine.

"Leah has something she wants to show me, and I have something I want to show her—see you guys later."

As soon as they entered Tom's room, Tom held Leah's hands above her head and pushed her against the wall, almost mounting her there. He kissed her and started opening her dress with one hand, holding her arms with the other, thrusting against her.

Leah was just as hot and made throaty noises back at him, liking his sexy forcefulness. Before she knew it her clothes were off, and Tom stepped back to drop his. He picked her up and threw her down on the bed.

Tom knew exactly what he was doing. He didn't make love like this to Jill. With Jill he moved like a thoughtful caretaker, cherishing her. With women he would never see again, he was comfortable engaging in more forceful, angry sex—which came across to the women as passionate. He grabbed Leah's hair and rammed her from behind as he fondled her breasts. Leah screamed at the top of her lungs when she came.

Tom felt a pang of guilt that Jill wasn't by his side. But it wasn't the first time he'd felt this way, or the first time he'd betrayed her. The room was dark, with thick drapes shielding the bright desert sun. Tom and Leah fell back asleep.

The housekeeper opened the door with towels, and Jill followed her into Tom's room. Having acted on her suspicions, she was still surprised to find him in bed wrapped around a nude redhead—and unprepared for the reality of the painful sight.

"No, oh god, no!" she screamed.

Tom's Meeting:

"Man, I fucked up." Tom paced along the back of my wall office with his hands on his hips. "I'm going to lose her. She's dating some stockbroker now and she's happy!"

"Do you want her back?" I asked.

He sat down in a chair and the energy seemed to drain out of him.

"I've got to let her go. I want her to be happy," he said. "But Jill was always there for me—and I'm going to look for a girl just like her when I'm ready."

"That's going to take time and hard work if you want to keep her," I said.

"Tell me how I fix me," he said. "I don't want to screw up another relationship with a woman I really care about."

"Tom, you're already aware of some of your issues, just commit to the process as we talk through a number of losses in your life, then keep yourself open to some new thinking and realizations."

"Okay," he said. "I'll be here. I want to do this."

Tom's Background:

Tom's story became critical at the loss of his brother Tony. Tom was shattered, but his parents offered no help—they made it worse. His mother abandoned the family, and Tom's father abandoned Tom by deadening himself with alcohol. Tom was left alone with his grief and guilt.

Tom's Assessment:

Because Tom has never dealt with the loss of his brother, mother, and father, he is dealing with bereavement, abandonment, anxiety, and depressive issues all at once.

After an intense assessment where he was given multiple psychological tests, it was determined that he was suffering from all of the above. After numerous Cognitive Behavioral Therapy sessions, Tom is well on his way to recovery.

Following months of hard work, Tom was able to overcome his anxiety and depressive issues through therapy sessions—without the help of prescription medication. Tom no longer suffers from panic attacks. He relayed that he no longer feels a void in his life and thinks someday he will be able to have a committed monogamous relationship with a partner. He no longer torments himself over the loss of his mother, and he has learned not to blame himself for the death of his brother.

In addition he has been in contact with his father, who has been sober for the past four years. He went to several couples therapy session with Jill. She tried to forgive Tom for his cheating but found she couldn't.

Tom says Jill has moved on with her life and he's happy for her—she deserves happiness. He says he just wasn't ready for commitment at the time because of all his emotional baggage. He now sees that his cheating was an attempt to outrun abandonment and grief issues.

Tom's Recommendations:

- Tom should take his time before he pursues another relationship with a woman. He needs to be sure he can deal with life's stressors.
- Tom should get a substance abuse assessment

and if indicated enroll in a substance abuse abstinence program.

- Journaling about the loss of his brother could be beneficial to Tom.
- Continuing with cognitive behavioral therapy can help him with his depression and anxiety issues.
- Tom can taper off his Valium.
- Relaxation exercises will help Tom prevent a recurrence of panic attacks.
- He should continue with individual therapy to talk about the losses that led to his abandonment issues.

Tools: Are You an Abandoned Cheater?

1. Are you constantly fishing for compliments because you feel insecure or inadequate?
2. Do you go to excessive lengths to get support from others?
3. Do you have sex often to feel better or because you feel hopeless or are preoccupied with finding attention from someone when you're alone?
4. Have you experienced a shattering loss in your life—a death or abandonment you know you've never worked through?
5. Are you an overachiever who is always trying to prove yourself to others? (For example, Tom trying to prove his worth to his father.)

6. Are you always trying to fill a void you never seem to be able to fill? For example, constant attention from various women or men.
7. Do you urgently seek another relationship as a source of support when one relationship ends?
8. Do you have a problem letting go of bad habits and use them to self-soothe? For example, drinking and/or having affairs even though you know that neither of these will fulfill your needs?
9. Do you go to excessive lengths to obtain support from others?
10. Do you feel uncomfortable being alone?
11. Do you feel excessive guilt, which never completely goes away?

If you've said yes to five or more of these questions, you may be an abandonment cheater with dependency issues.

19

REVENGE CHEATER

Ashley (Previously in author's preface)

"Mr. Riley, this is, Cara," the voice on the phone said.

"Hold it, sorry, I can't hear you, this place is noisy. I'll go outside," he said. Rick was in his softball uniform and about to celebrate his team's league victory in a little strip mall bar.

"Okay, it's quieter here, who is this?" he asked.

"Cara. Cara Jones, your babysitter," she said.

"Are you at our house, Cara? I thought that Ashley was staying home with the kids tonight," he said.

"No, sir, she went out with her friends tonight."

"Her friends? What friends?"

"I'm not sure, Mr. Riley, but my Mom said that I have to be home by 10:00 tonight or I will never babysit for you again. It's almost 10:00, sir," she said.

"Did you call, Ashley? She knows this is my softball night," he said.

"Yes, Mr. Riley. She doesn't answer her phone, I've tried several times," she said.

"Can you come home, so I can be home on time, sir?" she asked.

"Yes, Cara, I'll be there shortly," Rick said.

"Okay, bye," Cara said.

"Damn!" Rick punched the wall as he hung up the phone.

"I got to go home. See you guys later," Rick said.

"Man, are you getting snagged by your ball and chain? Tell Ashley to ease up," Rosco said.

"No, this time it's my babysitter. Don't drink all the beer in case I can come back," he said.

"Hey, if it helps man, if I had Ashley to go home to every day, I'd be a happy guy," Roscoe said.

Rick body checked Roscoe against the wall, not hard, but overly aggressive for a fellow teammate.

"What did you mean by that Roscoe?" Rick said.

"Lighten up. Ashley's an attractive woman. It was a compliment," Roscoe said.

"Yeah, that's it?" he asked.

"Yeah." Roscoe said.

Rick liked all the guys on the team, except Roscoe. Rick felt competitive with him—and jealous of him. Roscoe was attractive, had a good job, and always had his choice of women. Rick thought Roscoe acted like an arrogant stud.

He hated how Roscoe wanted the attention of every woman in the room. He wanted every head to turn to him—and they did too. Rick also didn't like that he had flirted with Ashley a couple of times. Like he needed Ashley's head to turn.

"Yes. I think you're a lucky guy, is that a problem for you?" Roscoe asked.

"What, do you think she's better than me?" Rick asked.

"Yes, less threatening and prettier..." Roscoe started.

"There's always prettier. I've seen lots of hotter girls than Ashley around here," Rick said.

"Nicer, did I say nicer? Let go of me Riley, I'd like the cigarette machine out of my back, and I wouldn't want someone in the bar to think we aren't team mates that just won a series together," Roscoe said.

"Okay, I got to go," Rick said. Rick left the bar but several other teammates in the bar watched the confrontation.

"He's an asshole," Roscoe said.

"No, he's just on the edge. His wife and he have been going to counseling," a teammate said.

"Marriage counseling?" Roscoe asked.

"Yeah," his best buddy confided.

"Is it doing any good?" Roscoe asked.

"Why do you want to know?" he asked.

"Because if she gets a divorce, I'd be first in line," Roscoe said.

"Ask her, there's Ashley now."

"Hey, Ash," Roscoe said as he sauntered over.

"Hi, Roscoe. Congratulations on your win," she said. "I heard you were Most Valuable Player."

"Yes, if you need a Player, I'm your guy," he smiled and stared right into her eyes.

She swore she saw twinkles coming from them.
"You're so sexy when you smile like that," she said.

"Can I buy you a drink?" he asked.

"Yes," she said.

"How about if we take that back booth there?" Roscoe asked.

"I'd like that," she said. "But first…"

She pulled a credit card out of her wallet. "Hey, bartender, I'd like to buy five pitchers of beer for the winning team," she said. "And give yourself a big tip!"

The team cheered for Ashley and three of the guys lifted her up and carried her for a lap around the bar to applause and attention. In a few minutes she had the best attention she had in a long time and she was sitting on the same side of the booth with Roscoe blocking her outside for her.

They chatted and flirted in the booth awhile and then the conversation turned more serious.

"I've always liked you," Roscoe said. "Are you happy?"

"Not really. Rick and I work on it, we're going to a marriage counselor, forgiving someone is not an overnight thing for me, you know," she said.

"Yeah, it wouldn't be for me either," he said.

"You're just a confirmed bachelor though aren't you, Roscoe?" she asked.

"No, I could fall for the right girl," he said.

"What would the right girl be like for you?" she asked.

"She'd be everything you are, and nothing you aren't," he said. "Want the truth?" he asked.

"Yes," she answered.

"If I could pick my girl, then you'd be a free woman and you'd be seeing me."

"That's just talk, Roscoe. We're in a bar and I believe you're flirting," she said.

"I am," he said. "Only these aren't lines, Ashley. I've always liked you and I know I could fall in love with you. You're beautiful, sexy, and I want to hold you and never let you go. I've even dreamt about you."

"You have?" she asked.

"What happened in the dream?" she asked.

"Rick was out of the picture and you were mine," he said. "And I was making love to you. It was hot and passionate, too."

"You know the hot and passionate part?" she asked.

"Yes," he said.

"So when is the very earliest I could try this out?" she asked softly stroking his thigh under the table.

"Check please," he said. In a moment Roscoe paid his tab and Ashley walked out of the bar with Roscoe right next to her. The teammates all knew what was about to happen and there was silence and stares from the team as they watched Ashley and Roscoe go out the front door together.

"Holy shit. That sure complicates the play-offs for us. We need Rick as a pitcher and we need Roscoe on 1st base," a teammate said. The team talked about the pros and cons of staying out of it, or telling Rick.

Some said, "Let's not get involved. The bigger the deal is, the harder for him to overlook it. He has kids." Others said, "Maybe he can stop it." "If he goes to stop it, what if it ends with a knife or a gun?" They all debated it for an hour, but by midnight someone decided to call Rick and tell him.

"She what?" Rick yelled. "I've been waiting all night for her."

Rick left the kids sleeping and drove 2 miles over to Roscoe's to knock on the door. Ashley's car was in Roscoe's driveway.

Rick pounded on the door, "Ashley, get home, you have two kids at home waiting for you. Get home, right now,"

There was no answer.

"Roscoe, you son of a bitch, answer this door, right now," Rick yelled.

Rick's cell phone rang and he answered.

"Rick, Roscoe and I are having a lovely time getting to know one another, much like what you have done in the past with others to me. I'll be home tomorrow and we can talk about this."

"Meanwhile, I have a man who likes my figure, thinks I'm hot, and can't wait to bed me, and I'm going back to bed, Rick. I know you may think this is about revenge because of all that you have done, but it feels wonderful. You've had your time, let me have mine. If you knock again on the door, we are calling the police."

Ashley's Meeting:

Ashley walked into the office and sat on the opposite side of the couch from Rick. The two were not talking to one another and I could sense the emotion between the two was about to ignite.

"Well, Dr. Wood, Ashley decided to fuck one of the guys on my softball team and made sure that everyone

I know—knew it. I had to quit the team. The team I've played with for twelve years and taken State Champions for three years together. I can't go anywhere—I can't show my face. I am the laughing stock in town."

Rick was embarrassed. He tried to hide that he was wiping away a few tears as they streamed down his face. His hands were shaking.

"Why did you have to do it?" he screamed, "to humiliate me in front of my friends, parents, and my children? Was it really worth it? How can you just sit there unresponsive, when you just ripped my heart out? How can you be such a cold bitch?"

"Turnabout is fair play," she whispered. "You didn't worry about what your fucking around did to me, did you, Rick?" Ashley stared out my office window, looking cool and unaffected.

"Ashley, it is not uncommon for people who go through the trauma of infidelity to become detached," I said.

"I could tell Ashley was very detached from the interaction going on in my office and Rick. She was watching the good-looking chiropractor that works in my building get out of his Porsche.

"Ashley did you hear me?" I asked.

"Sorry, Dr. Wood were you talking to me?" Ashley asked.

Ashley's Background:

Ashley has a twin sister, Tisha, who would often get more attention from their parents. As they were growing up, her sister was more outgoing, got better grades, and earned more respect from her parents—and Ashley hated Tisha for that. Whenever Tisha got the extra attention, Ashley would find some way to get more attention from passive aggressive behavior. Her ploys would work. Usually her parents were unsure which twin did the underhanded tactic, she would get away with it, get attention, and one-up her twin. Ashley's underhanded tactics worked in college to win out one of the last places on a cheerleading team. And worked again when she stole Rick away from her twin sister, Tisha.

Getting Rick away from the relationship he had with Tisha was her best revenge for all the years that Tisha outshined her growing up—until she fucked Roscoe. After Rick ran around on her, she loved the sense of self-satisfaction with setting him up for the same fall that she had taken when he ran around on her.

Now what? They have both damaged each other, and can't see where they could possibly find their way back to one another.

Ashley's Assessment:

Although Ashley and Rick agreed to work on their marriage after Rick's cheating; Ashley was unable to get through the rage stage of infidelity. Due to poor coping skills when angry, Ashley's behavior was in a passive aggressive manner. She decided to show Rick that two can play this game and cheated on Rick as an act of revenge, to hurt him as he hurt her.

Ashley thought that cheating on Rick would make her feel better about herself and less angry with Rick. But it didn't work.

Ashley feels guilty about her infidelity with Roscoe and can barely look at herself in the mirror. Rick and Ashley say they are humiliated that they are now the town's gossip and their marriage problems have become so public. Ashley is even angrier at Rick because she feels like his actions pushed her into the affair. To complicate things further a younger woman at Rick's work has let him know she's waiting for him.

Ashley is cold and detached from everyone because she is unable to accept her poor choices. Ashley has to work on her self-esteem issues before she works on her marital issues and rebuilds the trust in her marriage.

Ashley's Recommendations:

- Rick and Ashley have more infidelity issues to work out and need to continue therapy.
- Rick and Ashley need to talk to the children and find out how much they know about the infidelity.
- Rick and Ashley would benefit from individual therapy to work on their own self-esteem issues.
- Rick and Ashley need to address the issue of infidelity with honesty.
- Rick and Ashley need to utilize their support systems without involving them in the infidelity issues.

- Rick and Ashley have to go out alone and talk about the infidelity and why it occurred.
- Rick and Ashley need to try to keep as many friends and family members out of their infidelity issues as it will only complicate things.
- Ashley needs to work on her detachment issues before they get out of hand.
- Rick and Ashley need to understand that they are parents and need to be adults that are accountable and responsible to each other and their children.

Tools: Are you a Revenge Cheater?

1. Has your partner cheated on you in the past year?
2. Do you feel an underlying hatred for your mate after the infidelity?
3. Do you have dreams or preoccupations about getting even with your spouse after they have cheated?
4. Did your significant other cheat with someone who was close to you?
5. Are you ashamed to go out of the house due to the infidelity?
6. Do you feel like you want to emotionally ruin your partner for cheating on you?
7. Do you fight non-stop about the infidelity with your significant other?

8. Do you feel insecure about your sexuality ever since your partner cheated?
9. Do you feel unlovable after the infidelity?

If you answered yes to four or more of these questions, you maybe at risk in becoming Revenge Cheater

20

THE ETERNAL YOUTH CHEATER

Caroline

Caroline Chase passed by the All You Can Eat Fish Fry Fridays 5-9 pm sign to slide into a booth with a small, sleazy-looking man. She wore large dark Gucci glasses and a scarf—she did *not* want to be recognized in the tacky restaurant by the Los Angeles airport.

"Hi, Caroline," Rudy said.

"Hi, Rudy," she said. "What did he pay you?"

"Five thousand a week."

"I'll double it," she said.

"Fine, I'll tell him you're shopping. I got pictures of you at Westwood Mall, I'll show you entering Nordstrom's and coming out with packages. I'll change the dates and times on the film so it looks authentic."

"Good."

"Now for your evening rendezvous, we have to get you in a theater or something, night activities—you know."

"The movies sound fine."

"I'll have to show your husband you're with a girl-friend at the theatre," he said.

"Okay, but can't you take a photo there and put my face on it?"

"It's harder. The dress, the jewelry, everything has to jibe with what you look like and what you own," he said. "He must seriously suspect you're cheating or he wouldn't have hired me."

"He's always suspected, Rudy. He's twenty-five years older than I am. He's suspected me for twenty years now."

"And have you cheated for twenty years?"

"Some of those years I was true blue. But lately, well, we're all getting older. I like the sport of it, you know? Someone younger and fun before things go blank for me."

"What do you see in that tennis pro?" he asked. "He looks like my grandkid."

"If you have to ask, you need to get laid by a young one. It's like dipping into the fountain of youth—every injection turns back the clock."

"I try to reminisce when I think I need that," he said.

"Memories don't do it for me. I need the action, get the juices going."

He squirmed. Caroline wasn't a girl anymore. She was a well-tended fifty-five who looked forty-five.

"I need to go meet Matt now," she said. "Do you have what you need? Next week I'll call you from a pay phone and you can take a few photos somewhere—an auditorium or something. I'll call you."

"Okay."

"Here's the ten K in cash," she said. "You won't double-cross me, now, will you?"

"I'd rather have people stay together. Better karma for me," he said. "Besides, fifteen K a week without being shot at is good in my line of work."

"I want to stay married, you know. He can't live forever and this will mean a lot of money to me when he goes—and he's had two heart attacks already."

"We'll keep you married," he said.

"Thanks, Rudy."

She left without ever taking off her dark glasses. She got in her Mercedes and headed north on Lincoln Boulevard, turning east on Pearl Street to a Santa Monica townhouse.

Following her back just a few cars was her husband, Garth, with his own photographer in the car. In moments they were filming Caroline kissing the tennis pro welcoming Caroline with a kiss at the door of the new townhouse she'd rented for him. It was all Garth needed. He cancelled all her credit cards, took her off his checking account, pulled all her jewelry and sold it to a pawnshop that was happy to make a house call. He changed the door locks, gave the title to her other car to the housekeeper, and wrote her off his insurance policies.

Though he hadn't planned his day this way, he found it a productive morning.

Caroline came out refreshed from her round with Matt. She smoothed her bangs and looked at her reflection in her car mirror.

Yep, I look at least a month younger. She picked up the phone to call Garth. Her cell phone was dead. *Oh well, I'll talk to him as soon as I get home.*

But she didn't.

In fact, she never saw Garth again.

The next two years Caroline was broke and relying on an attorney who took her case on contingency.

Her attorney wasn't very handsome, but he *was* very young.

Caroline's Meeting:

The first thing Caroline did when she came into the session was spend fifteen minutes in the ladies room arranging her hair and freshening her makeup. When she returned and sat down, she said she was having issues about death because both of her parents had passed away suddenly. She was scared the same thing might happen to her soon. She said her husband was a walking heart attack and her two sons were far too busy with their businesses to give her the time of day. She said when her husband took her money and left her, her young tennis fling disappeared.

"I guess I was delusional, I thought we really had a connection. I'm afraid I'll die a lonely widow no one cares about."

She glanced at her nails to see if it was time for a manicure.

"Oh, well, my attorney is way hot and young and he knows how much money is coming my way after the settlement. I'll be back in the game in no time."

She looked up from her nails.

"So, Dr. Wood, how old do you think I am anyway?"

Caroline's Background:

Caroline was raised by a single mother, Yvette, a New York Rockette who had an exciting life kicking her legs high. She had attention and status in New York, a good table at Sardi's, and applause when she walked across the street to the Carnegie Deli. She was a stunner, a recognized New York celebrity—for a while. She danced eight years before she turned an ankle and was put out to pasture for a younger girl, but Yvette was smart and married Arnie, a New York restaurateur with an all-star clientele. She was welcomed into the prestigious restaurant and signed autographs wherever she went. Often little Caroline would come along and watch her mother's star power.

"It's not forever, Caroline. You have to use your looks and youth while you can," she said. "Don't be afraid to take advantage, exploit them, do what you have to do. Beauty is a powerful thing."

By the time Caroline was four, she had manicures and took good care of her dresses. By junior high she was manipulating boys for practice. She liked to have as many as ten boys a week calling her.

She chose beauty pageants for her arena and won Miss New York when she was nineteen, placing fourth for Miss America the following year. She became recognized wherever she went. Now she was signing autographs and talking to young girls about world peace—which she knew nothing about.

A dashing hockey star snapped her up after her pageants and spoiled her rotten. The sex was athletic and good, but he cheated constantly and she wouldn't tolerate it. After they divorced it was hard not to gravitate toward strong young athletes.

Caroline's second marriage was to a New York Yankees pitcher who was sent down to AAA ball in Tampa. He superstitiously blamed Caroline, but in reality he was cheating with every baseball groupie around. He left Caroline broke and in debt. Then Yvette and Arnie died in a tragic penthouse fire. They left Caroline with no savings, no insurance policy, and unending litigation because the fire started in their penthouse.

At thirty-five Caroline was penniless and depressed. Then she met Garth, who offered her the world and financial stability if she'd be his wife. He was an interesting, smart sixty-year-old retired executive with hundreds of millions of dollars. Caroline said yes.

The trouble was, she found it hard to get excited about sex with someone so much older than she was. Feigning a bad back and his snoring, she slept in a separate room and prowled for younger talent.

Caroline's Assessment:

Even though she's still an attractive woman, Caroline won't just accept her aging body and fading looks. There was a day when she could turn every head in the room.

That day has passed, and she tries to hang on to her youth through sex with healthy young men. It's the only thing that staves off—for a while—her fears of dying or growing old alone and uncared for.

Having sex with men younger than her sons also gives Caroline a sense of power, since she can manipulate them with gifts and money. In addition, Caroline is using young men as her entertainment—what else does she have to do other than shopping and gossiping about the other women at the Country Club?

She has never had a job or any hobbies. She put all of her time and energy into finding an older rich man to pay her bills. She married wealth, and being with her husband makes Caroline feel old. Now she prowls for younger men and pays their bills.

Caroline's Recommendations:

- Caroline needs individual therapy to work on her core issues.
- She needs to work on her self-esteem, understand that she has other assets besides her looks.
- She needs to find purpose and meaning in her life. She should consider a volunteer job.
- She would benefit from group therapy so she could see how others perceive her.
- Caroline would benefit by journaling her feelings. This might help her with all her issues, including finding purpose in her life.

- Working out at least three times a week would help her feel younger and get her endorphin levels up.

Tools: Are You an Eternal Youth Cheater?

1. Do you find you're always looking for someone younger and hotter to fulfill you sexually, even though you're in a committed relationship? Are you uninterested in sex with your partner?
2. Are you bored with your partner because he or she is too old?
3. Have you had numerous surgeries to maintain your youth?
4. Does being around your partner make you feel older?
5. Did you marry your partner for money, security, and/or status?
6. Do you fixate on your appearance, panicking with every sign of aging? Do you fish for compliments about how young you look?
7. Do you feel a need to control a younger man/woman you're sexually involved with?

If you answered yes to four or more of these questions you may be an Eternal Youth Cheater.

21

ETERNAL YOUTH CHEATER
MALE

Larry

LegGoddess21 e-mailed Larry her phone number. He wrote it down on a scrap of paper he slipped in his top pocket, erased his browser history, and shut down his computer. He found his wife, Judy, in the kitchen.

"I have to do an errand at the shop, doll. Eat without me if I'm not back in—"

"Larry! You know Larry Jr.'s bringing Penny to meet us today!"

"Look, I'll try to be back in time." He gave her a peck and went into their five-car garage. He picked the BMW convertible and took off down the street. At the first city park he pulled into the lot and dialed LegGoddess21's cell phone.

"Hello," said a soft voice.

"Britney?"

"This is Britney."

"Britney, this is Larry Cook from SugarDaddie.com."

"Oh, hi Larry." She giggled. "I'm so happy you called."

Larry loved her voice and giggle.

"Those are some pictures you sent me, doll. Is that really you?"

"It sure is."

"You're a showgirl in Vegas?"

"I am. But we just got laid off from Jubilee," she said.

"Sorry. That show played a long time. So do you want to meet?"

"Can you come to Las Vegas?"

"I can be on a flight in an hour or two. We could have dinner tonight. I'll check into the Bellagio."

"Should we talk about what we want now?" she asked.

"We'll have plenty of time to talk tonight. I'll call you from the airport and confirm a time, figure about eight-thirty for dinner."

"I'll wear something special," she said. "What do you look like? You didn't send a picture."

"I'm a handsome, funny, entertaining guy, plus I'm loaded and generous. What's not to like?"

She giggled again.

"Britney, maybe you'd like to bring a friend. Your age. Your looks. You know, so you feel more comfortable. And I'll bring a friend too."

"Okay. I think Heather may come with me," she said.

"Great. Call you soon," he said.

Larry *was* a handsome, funny, entertaining guy—in 1985. Now he was a balding, slightly overweight, aging guy with money.

He hit speed dial. "Bernie? Pack your bags, we're going to Vegas."

Bernie had been Larry's best friend for years. They

shared more secrets than they could count. Larry started the BMW and went home.

"Judy, where's my bag, can you help me pack? I need to go to New York and find out what's going on with my Italian distributor."

"Can't it wait until Monday? Larry, Jr. and Becky will be here any minute. Dammit, Larry, she's his *fiancé*. It's a big deal."

"I'll meet her later."

Just then his daughter-in-law-to-be walked in the door with Larry, Jr. Larry, Sr.'s eyes bugged out. *What a rack!*

"Penny, this is my mom and dad," Larry Jr. said.

"Nice to meet you, Mr. and Mrs. Cook."

"Please call us Judy and Larry. So nice to meet you, Penny," Judy said.

Larry made small talk, but all the while he was checking her out and thinking, *Oh my, God. What I wouldn't pay for a piece of that!*

"Lunch is ready, let's sit down at the table," Judy said. "Larry's is packing to go to New York, so he won't be joining us.

Larry finished packing, ordered his plane tickets, then logged on to confirm that Britney and her friend should meet him in the lobby of the Bellagio at 8:30. He was just about to sign off when Penny walked by his office to go to the restroom, and he darted to the door to watch her ass. As soon as the bathroom door shut he took his bag downstairs,

threw it in the BMW, and headed to pick-up Bernie.

On the way to the airport, Larry said, "Bernie, you should see who my son's dating these days. A girl with the best rack I've ever seen."

"What's her face like? Did you look at her face?" Bernie asked.

"Sure, sure. Beautiful girl. Great ass, too."

"Did you get the hot tub room?" Bernie asked.

"Yeah," he said. "They comped us with a double suite. We need to gamble twenty grand a day."

On checking into the hotel, the men had their spray tans refreshed in the spa, then slipped into designer silk shirts with a few buttons open, Italian slacks and loafers, and each put on a thick gold chain.

Britney and Heather weren't beautiful showgirls, but they were twenty-two, which was the important part for Larry and Bernie. So they were happy. The girls were happy because Larry and Bernie took them shopping. Watches, perfume, boots, dresses, shoes, all paid for by the guys.

"Let's put your shopping bags in the room for safekeeping, then we'll go to dinner," Larry said. After dinner, they all came back to the suite.

The guys wanted to get in the hot tub. They'd dropped $3,000 on Britney and Heather, and the girls had been drinking right along with Larry and Bernie. In fact, Britney was loaded. Larry sidled up to her in the hot tub, but she was barely moving. Heather got out of the tub, went to her purse, and popped a pill.

When the girls passed out, Larry and Bernie laid them on the bed and went to sleep themselves. The next morning the girls and their shopping bags were gone.

"Wow, what a wild night that was," Larry said.

"Those girls were awesome," Bernie said.

"Oh, man, that Heather was crazy about you, did you see how she fell in your arms in the hot tub?"

"She's nuts about me," Bernie said.

Back home, Judy signed onto the Internet and saw Larry's AOL e-mail account still open. On impulse, she opened his inbox. There was a plethora of messages from women, all from the SugarDaddie.com website.

It's okay. I'm not surprised. She signed out so she wouldn't be tempted to look further. What was there to do? She was already married to him.

There was also nothing to do when Larry, Jr. came home no longer engaged.

"Mom, Penny gave me back my ring, and it's Dad's fault. He's a dirty old man—she said she feels uncomfortable around him."

"I feel uncomfortable with your dad too," she said. "And the sad part is, it never goes away. I'm so, so sorry."

Larry's Meeting:

Larry walked into my office ahead of his wife and leaned over my desk, invading my personal space.

"Hey, doc, you're a doll." He gave me a quick wink, rested his eyes on my chest, and tried to X-ray my legs through the desk. "I just got done working out at the club, I apologize for my attire." He was wearing a red velour sweat suit. He was in fairly good shape but really thick around the middle.

"He didn't work out, he goes there to leer at young girls," Judy said. Her hair looked expensively streaked and she had on a *lot* of jewelry for such a petite frame.

"Very nice to meet you, Dr. Wood. As you might gather, we want marriage counseling because Larry cheats on me. And I have proof."

She pulled out the credit card statement on which all the charges from Vegas had been made.

"Look at the receipts—these are from women's shops. Where's the merchandise?"

"I swear I was just gambling, I never meant to hurt you," Larry said.

"If you were just gambling you wouldn't tell me lies about where you were going. When is this going to stop? I can't live like this any more."

Larry was quiet for a minute. Finally he said, "I don't know Judy, I have a real problem."

Larry's Background

Larry's father owned a strip club, and his son was often there from as young as four years old. Sitting backstage with the costumed girls, he noticed the way his father looked at the strippers.

The strippers would talk to Larry when he was little, but they giggled and were so playful he thought it was because he looked funny. He felt self-conscious backstage with the girls, but his father kept bringing him to work, leaving him with them while he did the books. Larry saw that the young girls were sexual objects. If they tried to talk, he hid, then peeked and watched them from his hiding place.

Judy lived in a nearby apartment after Larry graduated from college. She was nice-looking but not pretty, and Larry wasn't handsome. They hung out together, enjoyed watching TV, going to movies, and eventually a sexual relationship. You might say they fell 'in like' with each other, a comfortable relationship that led to a nice enough marriage. Judy and Larry were sexually compatible, but he never felt with Judy the excitement he did when teenage young girls walked by.

At thirty-five, Larry had a small facelift and a nose job. He became a more confident man and found that sometimes women would look twice at him. By now Larry and Judy had a family, and Larry had virtually no sexual interest in his wife. He fed his ego through extramarital affairs as he fed Judy lies about his whereabouts.

The years rolled by and eventually his affairs ended, but he never stopped looking. Now he uses online opportunities to track down young girls, and his success allows him the financial ability to act on these connections. He doesn't actually have sex with the girls, but the contacts are sexual nonetheless.

Larry's Assessment:

Judy and Larry need to take a long, hard look at their relationship—there are many red flags when looking at this couple. Judy mentioned her husband's reaction toward Penny, which clearly embarrassed her, yet instead of addressing it, she dismisses it. She says she knows Larry frequently goes out of town to spend time and money on young women. But Judy chooses a passive aggressive stance toward the issue and spends Larry's money to 'get him back' and numb her pain.

Larry needs to uncover and assess the reason he wants to be around young, unobtainable women. He needs to feed his self-esteem and feel younger in a venue where he can do something he enjoys that isn't destructive to his family and, ultimately, to himself. He could join a gym and/or play tennis or golf. He could learn to be an ace dancer—with Judy.

Larry's Recommendations:

- Larry needs individual therapy—with a female therapist—to address the childhood issues underlying his obsession with young women he can no longer attract.
- Therapy can also help him understand what's behind his self-deprecating behavior and his objectification of women.
- Larry and Judy need to attend couples therapy sessions.
- Judy needs to talk about her feelings of shame and mistrust when she's around Larry and assess whether she'll ever be able to trust him again.
- Larry and Judy need to communicate their needs to one another.

- Larry will benefit from group therapy attended by men and women.

Tools: Are You an Eternal Youth Cheater?

1. Does your partner tell you that you view attractive women/men as sex objects? Have other people said this?
2. Do you seek out younger women/men even though you know they're not really attracted to you?
3. Do you want to be seen with a much younger woman/man—arm candy?
4. When you degrade women/men does it make you feel better about yourself?
5. Are you in constant fear of looking old? Getting old?
6. Are you preoccupied with thoughts of your death?
7. Do you suffer from depression because you can't do the things you used to do when you were younger?

If you answered yes to four or more of these questions you could be the Eternal Youth Cheater.

22

EMOTIONAL CHEATER
MALE

Ted

"How are things going today?" Tish asked.

"Fine, now that I'm talking to you, sweetie." Ted sounded like he was speaking to a child, but he was talking to a married co-worker named Tish.

"You looked so handsome today," she said. "I loved that bright tie on the white shirt with your tan. I would definitely buy from you. Did you have a good day?"

"I sold a contract to 3M, but it will be a long time before I get my commission," he said. "They ordered it for next year."

"Still, Ted, you don't sell to 3M unless you really know what you're doing. It takes someone with your experience and panache. You're so talented—everyone at work thinks so, you know."

"I didn't think I was noticed at all," he said. "How was your day?"

"Herb screwed up on the petroleum proposal big time. He quoted them forty thousand off and they say if

Mesa signs the proposal, Herb will have to make up the difference."

"Forty grand! Poor Herb." Ted lowered his voice. "What are you wearing now?"

"I just put on my white tennis shorts. Court time at seven-thirty."

"With your husband?"

"You know we play every Wednesday," she said.

"I hate that. I want to be playing with you. I've got a great serve."

"I'm sure you do, Ted. You have a great everything."

"Do you have to leave now?"

"In a bit, not right now."

"Good." He sighed. "Are you ever going to leave him?"

"I don't think so, Ted. Are you ever going to leave Betsy?"

"I don't think so." He knew Betsy was about the best partner he could have. She was a great mother who took care of everything, did a beautiful job of maintaining the family and their home, and she loved him. Deep down, he knew he still loved her.

"Well, then, there we are," she said.

"It doesn't change how I feel about you," he said. "I love you."

"I love you, Ted. I crave you."

"Me too," he said. "I better let you go for tennis."

"I hate to go."

"I hate you to go."

Betsy stormed into the room. "Who the hell were you talking to?"

"No one."

"It was someone, someone you sounded seductive with on the phone"

"It was just some girl selling magazines I was joking with. I told her no."

Ted had originally been attracted to Betsy for her fit figure, but she soon after he married her the kids started coming and she had no time for sports. When had she stopped being fun? She could cuddle with him to watch a movie, but she never said the right things to him to make him feel good about himself. Tish always said the right things—he felt great when he was with her.

Betsy grilled a great porterhouse steak and all the trimmings, a celebration dinner for Ted's new deal. Their three-year-old drew him a picture and their seven-year-old talked about going horseback riding for her first time. It was a lively dinner conversation— everyone laughed and had fun.

After dinner they went for a bike ride, read stories to the kids and put them to bed, then watched a romantic comedy nestled together on the couch Ted's thoughts kept returning to how much he loved Tish.

Betsy put on Ted's favorite nightgown and started a naughty dance for him, but Ted wasn't in the mood. He kept wondering if Tish was home yet. He could go out to the Circle K and give her a late call.

Ted's Meeting:

Ted visited my office after reading an article about me.

He was a slight, balding man in his mid-fifties. He

walked with a bit of a limp and wore large glasses.

"There's a woman at work I have a crush on," he said. "I want to have an affair with Tish, but I can't even make toast without burning it. I don't think I'd be clever about a real double life."

"Cheating is also hurtful to your partner," I said.

"Yes, if Betsy ever found out she'd leave me. I can't bear the thought of the family breaking up."

"Telling me about your desire to have an affair is a good idea, Ted. It's no longer a secret between you and your co-worker, which already makes it less fun. Once it's out in the open, you can confront why the fantasy of another woman outside of your marriage interests you. What do you like best about Tish?"

"She knows what I do every day, and she's excited about my job achievements. She has a kind, loving sound in her voice when we talk. I like that, too. She tells me she's thinking about me. That makes me feel important and loved. When I do something small she appreciates it and lets me know with enthusiasm," he said.

"If you told Betsy about a big pitch you're working on, and it was successful, would she be happy for you?" I asked.

"Of course. But she never asks me, so I figure she's not interested."

"Or maybe you just haven't been bringing it up because you share it with Tish?" "Yes, I guess that's true," he said.

"In fact, if you're honest with yourself, have you shut down your communication and sharing with Betsy?"

Ted stopped to think before he answered.

"Yeah, I guess I have."

"Do you realize, Ted, that a lot of what you get from Betsy could be going on within your marriage if you worked on communication?"

"Yes, I can see that," he said.

"Communication is key, Ted. Your wife isn't a mind reader."

"But now I'm not sure how to start again."

"I can help you with that," I said. "My advice would be to go home and tell your wife you need more affirmation for what you do at work and around the house. Once Betsy understands your needs, I wouldn't be surprised if your obsession with Tish doesn't disappear.

"I'm going to offer you some techniques that will help you get the ball rolling, Ted. Would you like that?"

"Yes," he said. "I would."

Ted's Background:

Ted grew up in a small Connecticut town. He came from a family of eight children and never got a lot of attention. As the third male, he wore hand-me-downs and learned to move fast at the dinner table or the food would be gone.

He was an average college student who dated very little until he met Betsy. She saw a handsome man with impeccable values. Ted saw a girl who took his breath away. They married after graduation and soon began a family. Ted was an average employee wherever he went.

A few years ago he got a job at which he excels. His

company pays him well and recognizes his accomplishments but in a matter-of-fact way. As for Betsy, she's stretched from meeting the children's needs and often takes Ted for granted. Ted's emotional affair with Tish fills the gap.

Ted's Assessment:

Ted has a romantic notion that he loves his co-worker Tish, who echoes his feelings, and they both fantasize about the magic they would have if they were together. Since they have an understanding that neither of them is going to cheat on their partner, Ted thinks his "affair" with Tish is harmless.

But it's not. It has permeated their intimate time and their bedroom as Ted unplugs more and more from his relationship with Betsy.

All Ted knows is that Tish makes him feel good about himself and that he can't get enough of her. Therefore he obsesses about her even when he is having what's supposed to be an intimate evening with his wife. His emotional withdrawal from Betsy threatens his marriage as surely as would an actual affair.

Ted's Recommendations:

- Ted and Betsy would benefit from couples counseling.
- Ted needs to share his day and communicate his needs to his wife.

- Ted needs individual therapy to work on his core issues, especially his self-esteem. He needs to learn that self-esteem can't be obtained from other people, no matter how complimentary they are.
- Ted needs to stay in the present when he's with Betsy. He needs to learn how to bring his thoughts back to his wife and what they're doing when a fantasy about Tish distracts him.
- He needs to appreciate Betsy and what he already has, then try for more with her. Communication, as always, is the key.
- Ted needs to tell Tish that their intimate talks have to stop because they're threatening his marriage.

Tools: Are You an Emotional Cheater?

1. Do you find that your partner doesn't meet your emotional needs?
2. Do you go outside your partnership to get your emotional needs met?
3. Do you feel undervalued by your partner? Or taken for granted?
4. Do you sometimes/often feel that if you had a different partner you'd be a happier person?

5. Have you found someone besides your partner to share intimate details about your life with?

6. Do you often complain to others about your partner?

If you answered yes to four or more of the questions you could be the Emotional Cheater.

23

THE QUIET CHEATER
FEMALE

Mary

Mary's Meeting:

Mary had eagerly entered my office, but now that she was settled in her seat, she looked down and said nothing. Finally she blurted out the reason for her visit.

"I'm about to cheat."

"But you haven't had the affair yet?" I asked.

"No, but I want to."

"Why?"

"Our handyman, Melvin, is so nice. He smiles at me, and he's got this mischievous twinkle in his eyes." She looked mischievous herself as she said this.

"Did he tell you he wants to have an affair?" I asked.

"No, but I think he would," she said.

"What has he said to make you think he would?"

"Well, he's charming and he inkles to me," she said with a smile.

"Inkles?"

"You know, sexual innuendos," she said. "He says

things like how much he likes my tiny little buns I brought to the church picnic." She giggled like a young girl.

"Oh, and you didn't bring tiny buns, he's talking about your figure?" I asked.

"Well, I did bring tiny little buns, but it's the way he says it. His eyebrows go up and down and he always calls me beautiful," she said. "He says, 'Good morning, beautiful.' He tells me how gorgeous I look every day."

"I'm glad we're talking about this," I said. "Do you think the risk of hurting Fred after forty years of marriage is worth the brief fun of an affair?"

"No, I'd never want to hurt Fred."

"Mary, you checked on your profile that you and Fred have poor communication skills." I said. "Do you feel you have a part in the communication breakdown?"

"I don't know," she said. I thought I'd better point the finger in the other direction to get Mary to open up.

"What does Fred do wrong?" I asked her.

"Well...he's thoughtless. For instance, in forty years, he's never once bought me roses for Valentine's Day."

"So every year you tell Fred you want roses for Valentine's Day and he lets you down?"

"Yes. I mean, no. I mean I don't *tell him* I want them. I want him *to want to give them* to me. He should just know this. It goes without saying."

"Maybe he'd want to give you flowers on Valentines Day if you told him that's what *you* want," I said.

"When you put it that way, it makes it seem like the ball is in my court," she said.

"It really is, Mary. When you have a want, a desire, or need you want your mate to fulfill for you, you need to communicate it to your partner. Men aren't psychic. You have to tell Fred what you need from him in your relationship."

The next day when Fred came home for lunch, Mary was ready. She'd practiced what she was going to say so often that the words easily rolled off her tongue.

"Honey, I know it's not a special day, but I was thinking a bouquet of roses would look very pretty in the entry. If you think of it, would you pick me up some flowers?"

"The long stem from the flower shop, or the short ones from the gas station?" Fred asked.

"I'd like the long stem to fit our wedding vase," she said.

"What color?" he asked.

"Pink or yellow, something that catches your eye," she said.

Fred had never heard Mary ask for something so frivolous from him and he took it seriously. He went to the flower shop, told them he wanted their finest, and brought home two dozen long-stem sterling roses in a gorgeous arrangement with baby's breath and an iridescent bow.

Mary's heart was touched when she saw Fred coming up the walk holding the flowers for her.

"Ask me for anything and it's yours, honey," Fred said after he kissed her.

Mary realized she needed to get clear on her needs

and share them with her husband. In the meantime, she made sure Fred had the most amorous evening they'd shared in a long time that night. Fred learned that roses are worth the price he paid.

Mary's Background

Mary was born to parents who were hardworking farmers with old-school upbringing. They didn't spare the rod or spoil the child and thought well-behaved children should be seen and not heard.

As she got older Mary had a huge first love with a boy at school, but when he told her how he felt about her, she couldn't tell him how she felt. He took her response as indifference and soon paired with an energetic, outgoing girl. Mary thought her jealousy shameful and curbed her tongue again so no one would know how hurt she was.

Repressing her wants, desires, and feelings was a pattern that became entrenched, as she grew older and married.

Mary's Assessment:

Mary lacks communication skills not only with her husband but also with people in general. She has lived a very sheltered life in which she believes she has nothing important to say, so she often says nothing at all. Her self-esteem is critically low.

Mary has boundary issues and is not sure where her

unconscious adoption of someone else's values stops and her own values begin. Mary's fantasies about an affair with the handyman appeared after she convinced herself that Fred no longer loved her and would never want to please her.

Therefore, she subconsciously—and passive aggressively—chooses not to ask for what she wants. Mary knows that if she never asks for roses she'll never receive them. When she tries communicating with her husband Mary begins to discover a whole new stratosphere in which she can express a need and have Fred meet it.

Mary's Recommendations:

- Mary should take an assertiveness training course.
- Mary would benefit from the social interaction of group therapy.
- Individual therapy addressing the core issue of Mary's self-esteem would be helpful to her.
- Mary needs to develop her communication skills to the point that she becomes comfortable with them. She should also practice social skills with her therapist.
- Mary should continue to communicate her needs to Fred and reward him when he meets them.
- She should find some interests and hobbies that suit her lifestyle.

Tools: Are You a Quiet Cheater?

1. Do you find that you're unwilling to be involved with people unless you feel certain you will be liked?
2. Do you find that you have a hard time saying no to your partner?
3. Do you "ask" your partner to do things in passive aggressive ways? For example, you take out the garbage because you assume he/she won't?
4. Do you view yourself as socially inept?
5. Do you often feel self-conscious or insecure around your partner?
6. Are you afraid your partner will reject your need for affection?
7. Do you find yourself fantasizing about an affair with someone you think finds you attractive even though there's no reasonable basis for the fantasy?

If you answered yes to four or more of the questions above you may be a Quiet Cheater.

DR. WOOD'S WRAP

Cheating is nothing new. Cheating has been going on since the beginning of time, and it always, always hurts. So how do we cheat-proof our relationships and our marriages? Considering how high the statistics for cheating are, how can you avoid becoming one of those statistics?

I have found through my own marriage and through working with couples over many years that:

Communication is the single most important key to cheat-proofing your relationship. Make sure you communicate freely with your mate. Let him/her know your needs and listen with your full attention to his/hers.

Think of your relationship as a work in progress. So many couples work hard at their job, with their children, at the gym, on their homes, on committees, on maintaining friendships. Yet they never think of working on their partnership, which needs consistent maintenance as well.

Make your partner feel validated. Far too often I hear from the cheating half of couples that their partners don't make them feel good about themselves, so they find someone who does.

Make play dates with your partner and be playful. Many people say they cheat because they're bored with their partners or they no longer have fun with them. Fun is important, you're never too old to play, and a sense of humor can help couples keep a sense of proportion.

Listen to your partner carefully—listen especially to his/her needs. Take time out of your week to make sure you're meeting your partner's needs *and* to make sure your needs are being heard. A number of people say they cheat because their partner doesn't meet nor understand their needs, so they find someone who does.

Try to avoid possible triggers to cheat if you know that your relationship needs are not being met. All relationships have highs and lows. Don't let yourself be vulnerable to outside temptation during the lows. I can't count the times I've heard: "I wish I hadn't cheated— we were just going through a really rough time in our relationship."

Know your own limitations, vices, and weaknesses. If you're aware of them you have a choice to avoid temptation or limit yourself. If alcohol and men or women are your vices, maybe you don't want to mix the two. Again and again I've had people tell me they cheated after a few too many cocktails. Always watch out for the pitfalls that turn into a reason to cheat.

Explore activities you and your partner can enjoy together. From golf to a book club to campaigning for a political candidate, activities shared give you time to bond with your partner. Too many people say they cheat because they have little or nothing in common with their mate.

Always try to keep your sex life stimulating. Take time to talk about your partner's needs and to express your own. How many times a week does your partner need sex? If the two of you communicate about your sexual fantasies, what kind of foreplay turns you on, etc., your lovemaking will be much more satisfying.

If you've been cheated on, be honest with your partner if monogamy is the only relationship that will work for you. If you are feeling that your foundation is weak and you may be tempted to cheat, discuss the issue with your partner. Once it's no longer a secret you'll be less likely to cheat.

When you feel your foundation is slipping, get help before it's too late. I have counseled many couples who said they tried everything to get their partner to listen to them but couldn't get them to hear what they had to say. They ended up cheating.

Remember, the grass isn't always greener on the other side. You may well find that a new relationship isn't notably different from the one you left or comes with new problems. Many people who've left their partners for the man or women they cheated with tell me they give anything if they'd stayed with their partner and made the relationship work.

Take responsibility for your own issues and actions. Don't blame everything on your partner. Many people in therapy have told me it was their partner's fault they cheated, but cheating indicates that the system is breaking down, and both partners play a part in cheating.

Never forget to keep improving yourself and your lifestyle. The happier you are as a person, the happier you're likely to be with your partner. Never, ever think that your happiness will come from others. Many, many people cheat because they're unhappy with their partners, but often they're just projecting onto them the unhappiness they feel within themselves.

Finally, if your relationship is going south, always seek therapy as quickly as possible so you can cheat-proof you relationship. Most often my couple clients' major regret has been that they didn't seek counseling or therapy sooner.

APPENDIX

IS SHE/HE
CHEATING CHECKLIST

Part A (More Overt) Does your partner:

1. Always carry cash when he/she never used to?
2. Make withdrawals from the bank account with no credible explanations?
3. Go out with friends a lot more than usual?
4. Seem overly distracted when out with you or family?
5. Constantly check a cell phone?
6. Go to bed later than you?
7. Turn off the cell phone or turn off the computer quickly when you walk in the room?
8. Hide a cell phone from you?
9. Seem uncharacteristically happy a lot of the time?
10. Get really defensive if asked about a certain person?
11. Enjoy a certain hobby or sport he/she was never interested in before?

12. Texts more than usual and erases the text messages he/she gets right away?
13. Avoids having sex or being intimate with you?
14. Seems distracted much of the time?
15. Goes out with friends that you have never met?
16. Seem overly defensive if you ask what they did that day or evening?

Part B (More Covert) Has your partner:

1. Been buying new panties or underwear?
2. Started showering after being out with friends?
3. Gotten in really good shape in a brief time frame?
4. Started shaving genitals or waxing private parts out of the blue?
5. Been reading books on great sex and never asked you to check them out?
6. Been putting out a different sexual scent after being with "friends"?
7. Been spending excessive time grooming and dressing well when going out with friends?
8. Been avoiding a kiss or intimacy after coming home later than usual?
9. Been smelling like perfume or aftershave when he/she walks in the door after an evening out with friends?

10. Are going on more work trips?
11. Are spending more time helping out "friends or relatives" with projects?
12. Are avoiding your friends and family to do their own thing?

GROUND RULES FOR COUNSELING WHEN YOUR PARTNER CHEATS

Cheat-Proof your Relationship

- Your partner may want to make your relationship work yet be fearful to confront his/her shortcomings. Don't take this as a sign that your partner doesn't love you or doesn't want to make the relationship work. Be persistent in making sure the two of you get therapy.
- Always be honest and open with your therapist and your partner. Remember that there has already been a betrayal, so you need to rebuild your foundation.
- Be ready to admit that your system is broken and needs to be fixed.
- Try to avoid blaming or pointing fingers, as this will cause your partner to close down.
- Both of you need to acknowledge the weaknesses in your relationship.
- Be honest about your emotions. You may be

fearful that the cheating will happen again. Talk about the fear.

- There will be anger. Be open to working through this anger with your partner.
- Remember that if you want the relationship to continue, it will take hard work on both your parts.
- Look at the cheating and your partner's willingness to work with you on cheat-proofing your relationship as a new start to a healthier, happier union.
- Try to involve as few people as possible. All your friends and relatives do not need to know. Save the venting for your therapist.
- If you have children, *do not* involve them in the infidelity issues.
- It's hard to trust a cheating partner again, but if you forgive and trust, that will strengthen his/her resolve not to cheat. And the therapy sessions can help you trust.
- Become a strong force together. If you and you and your partner love each other, don't let the cheating pull you apart. Use this as a time to become united and build a stronger, more solid relationship.
- Try to make a habit of showing each other the respect you both deserve.
- Realize that it may take a while for your sex life to become active again.

- Work openly on this issue with your therapist, who can provide activities to help get the two of you back on track.
- Discuss your mutual needs with your partner and the extent to which each of you is meeting them.
- If you're the cheater, understand that your partner is going to feel insecure in your relationship at times. Try to diminish those fears as much as possible with any reassurance your partner needs.
- If you're the cheater, work with a therapist on understanding your desire to cheat.
- Whether you're the cheater or were cheated on, know that cheating may be a call for help in changing your relationship.
- Learn how to fight fair. Fights that exchange blame will only push your partner further away.
- Just about any relationship is salvageable if both parties are willing to work on it together in a dedicated, faithful, forthright manner.
- Be open to cheat-proofing your partnership with the help of your therapist. It just may take your relationship to a whole new level.

WHEN IT'S TIME TO RUN

Warning Signs for Leaving Your Cheating Mate

- If you've been dating exclusively for less than six months and your partner has already cheated on you, he/she may not feel committed to your relationship.
- If your partner has already cheated on you with a previous partner, he/she may not be over that person.
- If your partner hangs out with friends who cheat on their partners, take it as a warning sign.
- If your partner has promised to never cheat again yet keeps cheating, face the fact that you've got a cheater for a partner. Accept it or get out. And if you accept it, know that you're letting yourself in for a world of heartache, no matter how unthinkable life without him/her may seem. For that reason, my advice to the partner stuck with a cheater is get out.
- If your partner comes from a dysfunctional family where cheating was the norm and is

unwilling to go to therapy, the chances of cheat-proofing your relationship are virtually nil. It's time to get out.

- If your partner blames the cheating on you—your inability to satisfy him/her in bed, your nagging, whatever—the prospects for cheat-proofing your relationship are dim to nil. Unless he/she agrees to therapy, get out.

- If your partner admits cheating on every partner he/she has ever been with, you've got a cheater. Get out.

- If your partner sees nothing wrong with cheating, get out.

- If your cheating partner is demeaning or abusive to you and refuses to get counseling *and* therapy, get out.

- If your cheating partner constantly degrades the opposite sex and won't agree to therapy, get out.

- If your cheating partner has a highly addictive personality and won't get therapy, get out.

- If you know your partner is overtly trying to hurt you by cheating on you, get out.

- If your partner has no desire to cheat-proof your relationship after cheating on you with your best friend, roommate, sibling, etc.? Get out.

- If your partner looks at cheating like it's a game or a sport? It's therapy or get out.

- If your partner agrees to get therapy after getting caught cheating on you but then refuses to make the therapy commitment to cheat-proof your relationship, get out.

- If your partner shows no signs of remorse after cheating, his/her cheating may be pathologically driven, in which case even with therapy you may need to get out.

POST CHEATING GUIDE—
TIPS TO REMEMBER:

1. Never make rash decisions when infidelity is first confronted. Emotions are too out of control at this point.
2. Take some time away from one another, if needed.
3. Don't tell friends or relatives something you may later regret.
4. Know that the system is broken at this point and realize that the two of you need to eventually decide if it's worth fixing.
5. Take into consideration children, extended family, and friends, but involve them as little as possible. This is your problem and your partner's, not theirs.
6. A therapy office would be the ideal place to discuss the cheating, because you'll have professional input.
7. Talk openly with your partner about your feelings.

8. Know that this too shall pass. The two of you will emerge stronger or the relationship will end and you'll move on.

9. Try to avoid name-calling and blaming. It won't help.

10. If an argument transpires and becomes physical, abort the discussion and get away from one another as quickly as possible.

11. Try not to feed any guilt, jealousy, or rage you're feeling. These emotions have negative effects on your psyche.

12. Try to keep your discussions about the cheating within the therapy sessions.

13. Never degrade your partner in front of the children, no matter what he/she has done. If you do, this will only cause further harm to the family.

14. Know that if you go to therapy and work on the issues together, at least you can say you tried.

15. As a therapist I have seen many couples become stronger than ever after infidelity. If they can, you can too.

16. Though years of practicing psychology, I have seen many marriages actually saved following infidelity. Be open to this possibility.

17. Know that getting your relationship cheat-proof will take a lot of hard work and introspection as a couple.

18. Stay positive in your thought process. Imagine the relationship the way you dream it should be.

19. Make the cheating crisis a new beginning for the two of you rather than a bitter ending. If that's what you both want and you work together on it, you can have it.

REFERENCE LIST

Christensen, Al, & Jacobson, N. S. (1999) *Reconcilable Differences*. New York: Guilford Press.

Dinkmeyer, D., McKay, G. D., & Dinkmeyer, D. (1997). *The Parent's Handbook: Systematic Training for Effective Parenting* (STEP). Circle Pines, MN: American Guidance Service.

Doherty, W. J. (2001). *Take Back Your Marriage: Sticking together in a World that Pulls Us Apart.* New York: Guilford Press.

Enright, R. D. (2001). *Forgiveness is a Choice: A Step-by-Step Process for Resolving Anger and Restoring Hope.* Washington, DC: American Psychological Association.

Gottman, J. M, (1999). *The Seven Principles for Making Marriage Work.* New York: Three Rivers Press.

Liberman, G., & Lavine, A. (1998). *Love, Marriage, and Money: Understanding and Achieving Financial Compatibility Before—and After—You Say, "I Do".* Chicago: Dearborn Financial Publishing.

McCarthy, B., & McCarthy, E. (2003). *Rekindling Desire: A Step-by-Step Program to Help Low-Sex and No-Sex Marriages.* New York: Brunner-Routledge.

McGraw, Dr. Phil. (2000). *Relationship Rescue.* New York: Hyperion.

McGraw, Dr. Phil. (2000). *Relationship Rescue Workbook: Exercises and Self-Tests to Help You Reconnect With Your Partner.* New York: Hyperion.

Solomon, S.D. & Teagno, Lorie J. (2006). *Intimacy After Infidelity: How to Rebuild & Affair-proof Your Marriage.* California: New Harbinger.

Subotnik, R.B. & Harris G. (2005). *Surviving Infidelity: Making Decisions, Recovering from the Pain 3rd Edition.* Massachusetts: Adams Media.

Finding a Therapist Near You

American Psychological Association
www.apahelpcenter.org

Psychology Today
www.psychologytoday.com
American Association for Marriage & Family Therapy
www.therapistlocator.net

Australian Psychological Society
www.psychology.org.au

British Psychological Society
www.bps.org.uk

ABOUT THE AUTHORS

Dr. Denise Wood, M. A., Psy. D.

Dr. Denise Wood is a doctor of clinical psychology who graduated with Psy. D. from Illinois School of Professional Psychology and is fully accredited by the American Psychological Association. She received her Master of Arts in Counseling & Psychology from St. Mary's University.

Dr. Denise Wood is the founder of Wood Counseling Services. She is a relationship counselor who is passionate about helping marriages and families; coaches executives on life, career, and family issues; and assists businesses with candidate selection.

She is the star of *Cheater-Chat Podcasts*, *Dr. Denise on the Street* on YouTube, and enjoys doing radio and TV broadcasting. She is currently at work co-authoring her next book with Colleen Hitchcock.

Dr. Wood is married to Dr. Jim Wood, a Shoreview, Minnesota surgeon and lives with her two children, Page and Nick, and their furry friend, Sir Barkley.

Colleen Hitchcock

Colleen Hitchcock graduated from Minnesota State University with her Bachelor of Science degree. She is an alumni member of Maui Writer's Conferences, Santa Barbara Writer's Conferences and other Writer's Workshops.

Hitchcock's suspense thriller, *Rabbit Heart* about a French temptress in 1891 London who excites men to death is published by Simon & Schuster. *The Spud Gun Chronicles, Lethal Words, The V.I.P., Earthshine, and Other Short Stories* is published by Leopard Spot Press. Hitchcock's poetry is published in many books including best-selling author, Tom Clancy's *Without Remorse & Executive Orders*.

She is the host of *Cheater-Chat Podcasts*, currently doing audio recordings of her writing, and co-authoring her next book with Dr. Wood. She lives in Minneapolis, Minnesota with SuperPuppy Nikki, a dancing Pomeranian, who can read minds.

INSIDE THE CHEATER'S MIND

Why He Cheats
Why She Cheats

Dr. Denise Wood and Colleen Hitchcock will be publishing two other books in 2011. For more information, please visit www.cheatersmind.com

Dr. Wood's professional website
www.DrDeniseWood.com

Colleen Hitchcock's professional site
www.ColleenHitchcock.com

Leopard Spot Press
www.LeopardSpot.com

To order a book by mail
Send a check or money order for $19.95
plus $2.99 shipping to:

Leopard Spot Press
7117 Cornelia Drive
Edina, MN 55435
(952) 920-3100

Purchase Additional Copies at
www.LeopardSpot.com

Download FREE Cheater-Chat Podcasts on iTunes